Flying Star

FENG SHUI

FOR THE

Master Practitioner

風
水

LILLIAN TOO's

Flying Star
FENG SHUI
FOR THE
Master Practitioner

element

Element

An imprint of HarperCollins*Publishers*,
77–85 Fulham Palace Road
Hammersmith, London W6 8JB

element™

and *Element* are trademarks of
HarperCollins*Publishers* Limited

This edition first published in Great Britain in 2002

10 9 8 7 6 5 4 3 2 1

A catalogue record for this book
is available from the British Library

Illustrations by PCA
Calligraphy by Manny Ling

ISBN 0 00 712957 2

Printed and bound in Great Britain by
Scotprint, Haddington, East Lothian

Lillian Too's websites are at:
www.wofs.com for her online feng shui newsletter
www.lillian-too.com for her online author website

Contents

PART TWO The 24 Mountains

PART THREE Time Changes in Feng Shui

PART FOUR Flying Star Feng Shui

PART FIVE Interpreting Flying Star Charts

PART SIX Advanced Work on Flying Star

PART SEVEN Changing to Period Eight

Appendix

Applying the Secrets of the Feng Shui Compass

THERE ARE MANY SYSTEMS OF FENG SHUI BUT THE EASIEST TO MASTER IS COMPASS FENG SHUI. THIS IS BECAUSE IT IS VERY PRECISE, REQUIRING ACCURACY IN READING THE COMPASS AND IN DEMARCATING THE SPACE BEING FENG SHUIED. COMPASS FENG SHUI TAKES THE GUESSWORK OUT OF FENG SHUI PRACTICE, AND ALL SERIOUS MASTER PRACTITIONERS OF FENG SHUI USE THE FENG SHUI COMPASS, OR LUO PAN, IN THEIR PROFESSIONAL WORK.

The Luo Pan is an invaluable tool. At first glance it is an intimidating instrument – it is filled with as many as 3000 Chinese characters, numbers, lines, and symbolic markings. The Luo Pans used by masters of feng shui are usually at least 9 inches (22cm) in diameter with over 20 concentric rings of numbers, characters, colors, and codes. These contain a wealth of secrets – secrets handed down from master to disciple for hundreds of generations. The Luo Pan contains enough feng shui secrets to fill many books. Today, the bright glare of 21st century attention means that these secrets are available to an ever-growing band of "disciples."

To those who want to learn how to use the compass to create magnificent good fortune for themselves and their families, the secrets of the Luo Pan are worth learning – especially since on closer examination it is not such a daunting instrument after all.

The Luo Pan, or Chinese feng shui compass, is exactly the same as any western-style compass – it is not a different tool. Both compasses indicate exactly the same directions. The Luo Pan, however, was the ancient masters' means of condensing all their feng shui knowledge into one instrument. Today, all the information contained in the Luo Pan can be reduced to simple charts and graphics that can be organized and presented in user-friendly formats. Then all you need is a simple western-style compass to get your bearings and your orientations.

This book is, in effect, your Luo Pan. All the information in the Luo Pan pertaining to Yang dwellings (that is houses of the living as opposed to grave sites, or houses of the dead) is explained here in detail and illustrated, where necessary, in easy diagrams. Practical examples are used to explain the more complex applications of the compass but as you turn the pages you will be amazed at how simple supposedly advanced feng shui can be. Do not expect to become a master overnight, however. The formulas of feng shui are easy to understand but if you want your practice to have real depth and potency you should use these formulas as much as possible. Repeated practical application is important in perfecting one's understanding. Superiority in application comes from experience.

The more you use the formulas the more profound your use of feng shui will become. And then you will begin to appreciate the amazing genius behind this 4000-year-old system of environmental science. You will realize as you start to understand the lines and markings of the Luo Pan that the feng shui masters use it for more than just measuring directions. They use it as an instrument for studying the cosmic flow of chi, or energy, in the environment.

The Luo Pan recognizes that all directions are relative. Directions do not exist without a reference point. All directions – no matter who uses them – can only be expressed in terms of a starting point. Thus the Chinese view the compass as a measure of flowing chi currents around a piece of property or a home. This is the starting point, and from this they use the compass to divide the space around it, so that the chi of every degree of space can then be analyzed. In the Luo Pan, 360 degrees is first divided into eight segments of 45 degrees each. These correspond to the primary and secondary directions – north, south, east, and west, as well as northwest, northeast, southwest, and southeast. These 45-degree segments have their corresponding attributes, elements, colors, numbers, and meanings. Just knowing the meanings of the eight directions enables any amateur feng shui practitioner to benefit greatly from the correct placement of doors, objects, rooms, and so forth.

Much contemporary feng shui practice concentrates on using the meanings of these eight basic compass directions to determine the arrangement of space and the placement of enhancers within the home. In this book we go deeper.

This is because these eight directions can be subdivided again to fine-tune the practice further. The Luo Pan divides each of the eight segments into three sub-segments of directions. This means that instead of having only eight directions, we now have 24 – each covering an angle of 15 degrees. The meanings of the Luo Pan are expressed according to these segments, which are referred to as "the 24 mountains." Each mountain covers an angle of 15 degrees, and each angle of direction contains a broad range of meanings that define the variables of the most powerful formulas of feng shui.

The study of the 24 mountains is therefore central to the cosmic chi being analyzed. A further refinement of direction takes place when we go deeper. This is because the Luo Pan – and especially the Three Harmony Luo Pan – also takes account of three different bases upon which the direction north (and hence all other directions) can be determined. The Three Harmony Luo Pan recognizes three measurements of north: true north (that indicated by the sundial), magnetic north, and Polaris north. So there are three measurements of north. Each of these measurements is 7.5 degrees apart – with magnetic north in the center – and each is said to be sitting on a parallel "plate." The Heaven Plate equates with true north, the Earth Plate with magnetic north, and the Mankind Plate with Polaris north.

The feng shui master uses all the formulas of the different plates, and hence the different measurements of north to analyze different aspects of feng shui – whether the analysis is of mountains and rivers, or the influence of time on one's feng shui. It is because of this that the Luo Pan has so many rings – each set of rings signifies the meanings, formulas, and applications of each plate.

Our task is made easier, however, because most of the formulas for Yang dwellings use the magnetic north of the earth plate, and this is what we will largely focus on in this book. I strongly discourage amateurs from even attempting to practice Yin feng shui. The Luo Pan contains more than enough hugely beneficial information on Yang dwellings to keep one fascinated for a lifetime. It is unnecessary and even foolhardy to dabble with Yin feng shui since this requires practical work in cemeteries and gravesites. Ugh! As I have a natural aversion to cemeteries I have always politely declined any offer to teach me Yin feng shui.

There are different types of Luo Pan

Each type of Luo Pan contains the attributes and variables of different formulas. Thus one type of Luo Pan can be used to study the impact of landforms – such as mountains and rivers or buildings and roads in today's city environment. Another type of Luo Pan is used to assess the quality of spatial and time dimension feng shui, while a third type combines the different plates of the compass that take account of three types of north. The Luo Pan is a very accurate and subtle instrument in that every angle measured in degrees of direction offers various interpretations and applications. Compass feng shui is based almost exclusively on measuring the luck of directions – both facing directions and sitting directions. Compass feng shui evolved from the trigrams of the *I Ching* placed round an eight-sided Pa Kua symbol, and it addresses the feng shui of both Yin and Yang abodes. As we are concerned with Yang dwellings, none of the Yin feng shui instruction manuals are included here unless they also apply to Yang abodes.

Today's environment is different

Application of Compass feng shui in today's environment should take account of how buildings, roads, towns, and cities have developed and changed over the centuries. The living environment of the 21st century bears no resemblance to that of ancient China whatsoever. So the circumstances and visual appearance of today's world is not at all the same as when feng shui first developed. The chi was not as complex then as it is today, when we have to contend with the added complications of electricity and telecommunications.

Man-made or man-induced energy flow across the earth has added vastly to the lines of natural energy, so the kind of chi that affects modern homes is very different from that which affected homes and buildings of the past. It is important to bear this in mind when using the secrets of the Luo Pan. We need to be sensitive to the new environment when practicing feng shui – especially the significance of modern structures that may affect the feng shui of abodes near them. Thus satellite dishes, water tanks, transmission lines, multi-level roads – to name but a few modern-day structures – simply must be taken into account since their presence in any environment has strong feng shui implications. The same also applies to neighboring buildings. When the feng shui influence of surrounding structures is analyzed then care can be taken to diffuse any hostile chi emanating from them, while enhancing any benevolent chi they may send. This aspect of compass feng shui uses the Sarn He' Luo Pan's mankind plate. Here the formula uses the "man" plate set of 24 mountains and their corresponding elements in order to study the meanings of all nearby buildings, mountains, and structures. This is a very valuable formula which Hong Kong feng shui masters are especially fond of using.

The exciting promise of the Luo Pan

The Luo Pan is the key to unlocking a veritable treasure trove of methods that can be used to bring big transformations in luck. Over the course of this book I will share some of the skills that have been passed on to me. These will help you to read and understand the compass, tell you how to use the formulas for installing cures against bad luck, and how to activate chi to create powerful protective energy for you and your family. Good feng shui always means being protected from premature accidents and death. Good feng shui ensures that your family and all the residents of your household are safe, secure, and stable. Living within the embrace of protective chi helps you avert accidents and overcome life obstacles.

In addition, good feng shui that comes from well-positioned enhancers brings longevity and good health, success without obstacles, wealth, and great relationships. When used in conjunction with basic principles of feng shui, compass formulas add a stunning dimension to this wonderful practice.

Feng shui assessment is always about reading invisible chi patterns that influence a property. These patterns can be felt and determined on site – things like the strength and direction of the winds, as well as the smells and lushness of localized vegetation. But chi is best read by using the compass. In the atmosphere of any place there is always a vibration that one can tune into. The feng shui Luo Pan can often pick up these vibrations. More important than the tool, however, is a mind-set that encompasses earth and sky, land and water, Yin and Yang, productive and destructive forces, and a solid knowledge of formulas and interpretations. It is the practitioner that picks up the vibes of atmosphere and environment, so also trust your own instincts.

The living universe is a multiple blend of a billion permutations. No two houses or properties are ever exactly alike, just as no single abode has constantly good or constantly bad feng shui. The nature of energy is such that it is always changing and evolving. So when using the compass it is always a good idea to take directions again and again. This ensures that the orientations of the land as well as the home are accurately read.

Chi is an elusive force

Chi is not easy to pin down so taking directions can be frustrating when the needle of the compass refuses to settle down. Be patient. Chi is like mercury, hard to grasp. One can study it, analyze it, live with it, embrace it, feed it, trap it, accumulate it – but it is foolhardy to take it for granted. So be patient and take your directions carefully from different angles. The key is to get the orientations of your home accurate and then Compass feng shui will amaze with fabulous and quick results.

There is a depth to feng shui that is very challenging. There are those who use instinct or some special metaphysical capability in their practice of feng shui. Others use assessment of physical shapes and structures to arrange their feng shui. Still others use a combination of different methods – I have seen a multitude of approaches used by different people with varying degrees of success. My perspective on feng shui is derived from the viewpoint of a user. I have used feng shui extensively, broadly, and boldly – in my work, my business, and my personal life – and it has given me the competitive edge. For over 30 years feng shui has been a good and dependable friend – and while I have experimented with different formulas, performed various rituals, and applied Symbolic feng shui in every aspect of my life, underlying all those has been my total reliance on the compass. My approach to feng shui has always been based on the compass.

Formula feng shui

I discovered Formula feng shui very early in my practice and long years of experience have made me very confident in its potency. Formula feng shui has never let me down. But, like everything else, practicing feng shui requires us to make decisions and trade-offs: which formula to use, which room to activate, whose direction to use, where to place the main door, and so forth. It is completely to be expected that one has to confront situations where the different formulas offer different recommendations.

In my experience, Flying Star formulas practiced in conjunction with Symbolic feng shui bring the fastest positive results. It is even better to combine flying star with Eight Mansions feng shui – especially in the arrangement and layout of interiors. In the 21st century many of us really only have control over the interiors of our abodes. Those who have gardens do have some control over their immediate exterior surroundings – but this control is usually limited. Therefore, Flying Star and Eight Mansions feng shui – which use directions and orientations – offer very important means of manipulating the way we interact with the chi of our immediate environment.

Compass Flying Star feng shui evaluates a property from the perspectives of time and time periods, but we must also never forget to use the Sarn He' landscape formulas as these enable us to analyze the impact of nearby buildings. Eight Mansions feng shui adds the personal dimension and from this formula it is possible to identify directions and sectors that are particularly beneficial or harmful to individuals.

Compass feng shui is very comprehensive

Compass feng shui incorporates the study of numerology (the meanings of numbers and combinations of numbers), the powerful symbolic effect of the five elements, the two Pa Kua arrangements of trigrams, as well as some hitherto very well kept secrets of the feng shui compass itself.

Many feng shui masters acknowledge Compass Flying Star feng shui to be one of the most powerful systems of feng shui that has come down the centuries intact. Because of its potency, and its great reliance on numbers analysis, flying star, like the Luo Pan, can be daunting. In reality, this method of feng shui analysis is not difficult – indeed, as with all of the other schools and principle methods of feng shui, it becomes very easy once you understand the fundamental basis of the formula. Good feng shui works very fast in making your space feel more embracing and more harmonious. Feng shui has the potency to bring an easier life of abundance. But the element of personal effort can never be over stressed. When feng shui brings opportunities you still have to work at making something of those opportunities. Feng shui does ensure there are fewer obstacles in your life. It does bring better, more fulfilling relationships as well, and there are greater successes and higher incomes awaiting your efforts … using the compass methods leaves less room for mistakes because the techniques are specific and precise.

It is worthwhile investing time and effort in learning Compass feng shui because once you know how to use the different methods, you will amaze yourself with how proficient you can become at this ancient way of living in harmony with the environment. Flying Star feng shui takes the guesswork out of feng shui. Eight mansions personalizes your practice. The compass enables you to get the best of feng shui at all times.

You do not need to invest in a Luo Pan – a genuine and authentic Luo Pan is expensive. The charts in this book have all the information and knowledge you require to practice Yang feng shui. What you do need is a good ordinary compass. If you live in seismic area (for example, California) you will need a heavy-duty compass to get accurate readings. Otherwise any compass should be adequate. If you wish, you might find it useful to get a compass with the 24 sub-directions marked in. Armed with the compass, the formulas, and a clear mind, you can start immediately. Good luck!

Secrets of the Luo Pan

1. ORIGINS OF THE LUO PAN COMPASS

AN AUTHENTIC CHINESE FENG SHUI LUO PAN IS ONE OF THE MOST BEAUTIFULLY CRAFTED INSTRUMENTS IN THE WORLD. IT IS AN EXTRAORDINARILY PRECISE COMPASS THAT CONTAINS A TREASURE TROVE OF FENG SHUI FORMULAS AND SECRETS. THESE ENABLE THE SERIOUS PRACTITIONER TO TAKE PRECISE READINGS OF THE ORIENTATION OF ANY BUILDING OR PROPERTY AND, IF THEY KNOW HOW TO READ AND INTERPRET THE MARKINGS, OFFER INSTANT DIAGNOSIS AND SOLUTIONS.

Feng shui afflictions take different forms under a whole mélange of circumstances and orientations. These afflictions can be caused by physical structures within the vicinity of the landscape, the orientation of the building's doors and entrances, or simply the energy changes of time. All these and more can be decoded from the information contained within the Luo Pan. The markings on the Luo Pan give immediate correlations of every degree of orientation thereby pinpointing to the user under which method or formula there might be a feng shui problem.

How did the Luo Pan originate?

A colorful Chinese legend tells of a beautiful Goddess, known as the Lady of the Nine Heavens, who gave the Luo Pan compass to the Yellow Emperor and revealed to him the secret knowledge of how to use this special tool. Using the Luo Pan, the Yellow Emperor succeeded in defeating his enemies. In the ensuing centuries the compass device was progressively enhanced by the Duke of Chou, his son King Wen, and his grandson. The knowledge of the compass was combined with that of the Book of Changes, the *I Ching*, and, in the process, concepts of worldly and divine clairvoyance were established. Thus was formulated what would eventually become the fundamental underpinnings of the science of feng shui, a combination of all the knowledge of heaven and earth. As a tool, the Luo Pan was used in unison with the *I Ching*, which had by then been condensed into the eight-sided symbol called the Pa Kua.

Each Kua of the eight-sided Pa Kua symbol represents one major direction of the compass. And on each side is arranged the eight primary trigrams. These trigrams are placed in different arrangements thereby creating the Pa Kua of the Early Heaven arrangement and the Pa Kua of the Later Heaven arrangement. Both these arrangements appear in all Luo Pans. At the same time, the Lo Shu and Ho Tu squares were discovered and the numbers of these two numerology sequences were also synthesized into the Pa Kua and into the Luo Pan.

As a feng shui tool, the Luo Pan has been in use since the time of the Yellow Emperor around 2700 BC. It was initially used as a compass for taking directions before being refined into a complicated instrument for analyzing the landscape. Basically the Luo Pan was used to decipher the directional forces of nature and their bearing on the luck of abodes and their residents. Through the centuries and under different dynasties of imperial rule, the practice of feng shui has waxed and waned, but the Luo Pan evolved to contain the different formulas developed by different prominent masters during succeeding dynastic rules. Feng shui masters through the ages condensed their valuable observations and discoveries into working formulas, and their precious knowledge was engraved into the Luo Pan, to be passed down to their disciples.

During the Sung dynasty the lineage of transmission of divinatory sciences from one recognized master to the next was carefully chronicled. These transmissions included feng shui. In those times recognized experts were highly esteemed and feng shui practice flourished. The next dynasty significant to the story of feng shui was that of the Ming dynasty. During this time, feng shui developed new styles and orientations – rules were simplified and mountains, rivers, and stones were reclassified. Time cycles of feng shui were said to have been "invented" at this time, with the introduction of the Sarn Yuan (three periods or three cycles) system. Each cycle lasted 60 years, made up of three cycles of 20 years. This was to eventually become the basis of the Flying Star system of feng shui, which is gaining increasing popularity today, perpetuated by masters of the Compass schools. Flying Star formulas found their way into the feng shui Luo Pan which, during the Ming period, also expanded from 17 to 36 rings.

In the late Ming, however, feng shui took on a bad name as "fake" masters and books were said to have become rather widespread.

For this reason later feng shui scholars were extremely critical of Ming-period feng shui. During the Ching period, the practices expounded by the Ming scholars were censured and as a result there was movement towards embracing the more theoretical texts of the Sung practitioners.

2. THE FENG SHUI LUO PAN TODAY

Today the Luo Pan and its rings of symbols, trigrams, numbers, and Chinese words is regarded as an indispensable instrument by professional feng shui consultants. In the same way that the abacus continues to be used by Chinese merchants who prefer it to the modern-day calculator, feng shui practitioners of the old school prefer using the Luo Pan to the modern-day compass.

Of the many different feng shui techniques requiring the use of the compass the most popular and influential are:

- *The time cycle techniques also known as Time Dimension feng shui. This incorporates the Flying Star, or Shuan Kong, method of feng shui analysis.*
- *The Three Harmony method which refers to the harmony between Heaven, Earth, and Man, as reflected in the Heaven Plate, the Earth Plate, and the Man Plate of the Luo Pan. This Luo Pan is very comprehensive and contains three sets of rings, each denoting one of the plates. This is a combination Luo Pan which has many Chinese words and is said to be the most complete as it also contains information on time cycle feng shui.*

The feng shui Luo Pan is first and foremost a compass for measuring directions. So the most important part of the Luo Pan is the magnetic needle and directional marking in the center. It is vital never to compromise on the quality of this central needle since so many of the nuances of good and bad luck depend on accurate compass readings.

To reiterate: the Luo Pan divides directions into 360 degrees around a point of reference. This is divided into eight main directions and 24 sub-directions. These sub-directions are referred to as the 24 mountains, and each mountain measures 15 degrees (360 divided by 24 equals 15). The rings that indicate the 24 mountains of the different plates are very important simply because many of the major feng shui formulas use the 24 mountains to express and demarcate good and bad luck orientations. So all Luo Pans have the 24 mountains.

The remaining rings, however, can contain a number of different formulas, as Luo Pans vary according to which master designed them. Even when they contain the same formulas they may be presented in a different way. The numbers and characters of the Luo Pan are therefore confusing to the uninitiated – until they are interpreted and explained.

I want to stress that you do not need to invest in a Luo Pan to become an excellent feng shui practitioner. It is important only to know how to use a compass and how to measure, use, and apply directions according to the formulas. So as long as you have a compass – any good compass – you can apply all the secrets of the Luo Pan.

If, however, you do wish to invest in a Luo Pan here are a few guidelines. Good Luo Pans are made with precision and care, and are best crafted from wood – they should never be made of plastic, cardboard, or paper. The face of the compass, i.e. where the rings are placed, is known as the heaven dial and this sits on a base made of wood known as the earth plate. The heaven dial or face of the Luo Pan is usually made of stamped copper plate. High-quality Luo Pans have clear, sharp, and well-crafted characters and measurement degrees, and they never rust. Examine it carefully to make certain it is made of good materials and that the compass in the center is accurate and of good quality. Choose a size you feel comfortable with. A medium-sized Luo Pan is usually sufficient to contain all the essential information. When you buy a Luo Pan you should take care of it, storing it properly, and keeping it away from electrical and metallic devices so the needle stays sound.

Here are further pointers to take note of when examining a Luo Pan ...

1   *Take special note of the needle quality. This is the most vital part of the compass, and is the single most expensive part of any Luo Pan. The needle must align accurately on top of the red line in the center of the compass. Never buy a Luo Pan with a cheap needle. Also remember that the needle is extremely sensitive to metallic objects so a large needle might be better than a small one.*

2 *The two red dots must be present and these should point north (the rat direction) while the point of the needle should point south (the horse direction).*

3 *Look at the accuracy of the axis cross. These are the two nylon threads that must cross the cardinal axis directly at 0, 90, 180, and 270 degrees of the heaven dial. There cannot be even the slightest deviation. If there is, the Luo Pan is deemed to be worthless.*

4 *Take note of the heaven dial, which must be clear and not blurred so that characters can be read easily.*

5 *Turn the Luo Pan on its earth base – it should move freely and feel smooth.*

6 *The earth base should be square as directions are often taken by pressing it parallel to the wall or door of a building – the four sides must thus be square and straight.*

Generally I would say that for beginners, and for those who want to practice Yang feng shui, the ring of the 24 mountains is the most crucial – and this can easily be committed to memory using an ordinary compass.

3. SPECIAL LINES OF THE LUO PAN

Before we go into the details of the concentric lines around a Luo Pan, it is extremely important to take note of the special lines that indicate inauspicious directions. These pertain to what are known as the cardinal death lines and the major and minor emptiness lines. (The phrase death lines do not necessarily mean death in a physical sense. It can also refer to loss, failure, and other extreme forms of bad luck.) One of the most well-kept secrets of Compass feng shui – previously known only to lineage masters – is that the facing directions of doors and entrances should never lie exactly on the lines that indicate the exact cardinal and secondary directions of the compass. On a Luo Pan these lines are easily identifiable – they are the lines that bear exactly north, south, east, and west, and northwest, southwest, northeast, and southeast. Thus if north is deemed to be the best direction for you and you wish to have your door face north, then you should make sure it does not face exactly north but rather a couple of degrees off exact north. This is true of all the four primary directions and the four secondary directions.

Kung mang, or emptiness lines, also spell misfortune and severe bad luck. There are eight major emptiness lines and these separate each of the eight main direction sectors – N, S, E, W, NW, NE, SW, and SE. There are also16 minor emptiness lines and these separate the 24 mountain sub-sectors in each of the eight sectors.

The inauspicious and dangerous lines of directions are as follows:

The death lines *are the cardinal directions bearing 90, 180, 270 and 0/360 degrees, as well as the secondary directions bearing 45, 135, 225, and 315 degrees.*

The major emptiness *lines are directions that are bearing 22.5, 67.5, 112.5, 157.5, 202.5, 247.5, 292.5, and 337.5 degrees.*

The minor emptiness *lines are directions that are bearing 7.5, 11.25, 33.75, 37.5, 52.5, 56.25, 78.75, 82.5, 97.5, 101.25, 123.75, 127.5, 142.5, 146.25, 168.75, 172.5, 187.5, 191.25, 213.75, 217.5, 232.5, 236.25, 258.75, 262.5, 277.5, 281.25, 303.75, 307.5, 322.5, 326.25, 348.75 and 352.5 degrees.*

If you discover that your house is facing a death line or a major or minor emptiness line, and you are unable to change the orientation of your door, one method of at least reducing the negative effect is to place some kind of metal decoration on the door itself. This can be a door knocker (the best are brass lion head door knockers) or you can also hang sword coins on the inside of the door. The introduction of a bit of metal is usually sufficient to move the chi so that the main door into the house no longer faces the death or emptiness line. Having said this, please note that if you are having a spate of enormous bad luck and you discover that your door is facing one of these lines then it might be a good idea to adjust the door slightly so that it no longer faces the dangerous line of direction.

Another little-known method is to transform your house into a "heavenly abode" by placing an altar directly opposite the entrance door. You will find that the Chinese like to place their altars here and it is said to be an excellent antidote for overcoming the affliction caused by facing a kung mang, or emptiness line. It is believed not only to deflect the ill-effects of emptiness lines but also to bring in auspicious luck instead. Irrespective of your religion it is said that once you introduce an altar, any kind of altar, the emptiness line gets broken.

In addition to death and emptiness lines, there are also certain directions that are referred to as Yin gaps, and these indicate problems in human relations for the residents. Doors that face Yin gaps cause problems between spouses and create family disharmony, marriage problems, and can even lead to eventual breakups. The Yin gaps are the direct centerlines of each of the 24 sub-direction sectors.

These deadly directions and Yin gaps bring secret afflictions to any building and, because of this, feng shui masters who know about Compass feng shui always check this aspect of any home or office before they do anything else. When advising on the design of new homes this is also taken into account. Usually compass directions are taken during the actual construction of any home to ensure that directions are properly read and applied.

Since the compass is affected by the presence of metal, it is important to remember that main doors are best when they are made of wood. If there is metal on the door this should be taken into account when checking the door direction during construction.

4. HEAVEN, EARTH, AND MANKIND PLATES

In Three Harmony feng shui we must differentiate between the three plates of the compass – the Heaven Plate, the Earth Plate, and the Mankind Plate.

*The **HEAVEN PLATE** moves faster than the earth plate and is usually 7.5 degrees ahead of it (to the left). Here the measurement of north is described as true north based on the sundial. The heaven plate is generally used to check the auspiciousness of water flows. Here we are referring to both the inflow and outflow of water. (The heaven plate is also referred to as the water plate.) However, these refer to the water flows for Yin houses i.e. the burial plots of ancestors in grave sites. It is believed in Yin feng shui that water is very powerful in determining the fortunes of descendants. The potency of this form of feng shui is almost legendary and even today there are still feng shui masters who undertake Yin feng shui consultation. This branch of feng shui, however, is not suitable for mass dissemination. However, it is useful to know that the Luo Pan contains many secrets of Yin feng shui and the heaven plate is an indispensable tool for practicing this field of feng shui.*

The heaven plate is also used to provide alternatives for the emptiness and death lines – for instance, if the direction of the main door falls on an emptiness line, some masters use the "heaven plate solution" by adding 7.5 degrees to the door direction to see if under the new plate the direction turns auspicious.

*The **MANKIND PLATE** is slower than the earth plate and is thus 7.5 degrees behind it (towards the right). The difference in measurement is due to the different method of establishing north. In the*

The seasoned wisdom of thousands of years has gone into the making of the *I Ching*. It is the most important of China's ancient books and Chinese philosophy – both Confucianism and Taoism – has its roots in this timeless classic. Known also as the Book of Changes, the *I Ching* goes back to mythical antiquity. It offers a view on the trinity of heaven, earth, and man, and this trinity underscores a great deal of feng shui theory.

Four legendary personalities are credited with the authorship and evolution of the *I Ching*: Fu Hsi, King Wen, the Duke of Chou (King Wen's son), and Confucius – the most famous of China's great thinkers.

FU HSI, a mythical figure associated with much of China's ancient wisdom, is said to have observed the heavens and the universe, the changing of the seasons, and the change from night into day, and from his observations invented linear representations which became the three-lined trigrams. The trigrams are the roots of the hexagrams which came later.

KING WEN, the forefather of the Chou dynasty (1105–249 BC), was the man credited with the invention of the 64 hexagrams. He did this by doubling the trigrams from three lines into six lines. King Wen spent a great part of his life in prison before ascending the throne, and during that time he appended judgments to the hexagrams which became the ground work for what was later to evolve into the great wisdom of the *I Ching*.

THE DUKE OF CHOU, King Wen's dynamic son, authored the texts which were later to become the individual six changing lines of the hexagrams. He assigned meanings to them as and when they changed from Yin to Yang, thereby manifesting as broken or unbroken lines and vice versa. The Duke of Chou's contributions were entitled the Changes of Chou, and these subsequently came to be used as oracles. These changes, which are contained in a number of ancient texts, altered the complexion of the *I Ching* quite substantially and expanded it into a book on divination. This was the status of the book when Confucius come upon it.

CONFUCIUS devoted his life to studying the texts, the judgments, and the images of the *I Ching*. A great sage, he and his disciples also expanded its scope with a series of masterful commentaries. A great deal of literature about the book flourished during this period, and large portions of this were incorporated into the modern day *I Ching*.

Flying Star Feng Shui for the Master Practitioner

The I Ching *and modern science*

There have been major discoveries made concerning the similarities between the lines of the hexagrams and the binary code of numerations. The latter is the foundation of computer technology, so the similarities offer tantalizing potential for speculating on the relationship between the lines and modern technological breakthroughs.

The broken and unbroken lines correspond to the dots and dashes of the binary code exactly. This alone is an amazing discovery and it surely cannot be a coincidence. Scientists have also discovered that the 64 hexagrams of the *I Ching* correspond exactly to the 64 DNA genetic codes that are the basis of all life on the planet. It is thus possible that in the *I Ching* lie the hidden meanings to life's existence.

What has been accepted for hundreds of years, however, is that the *I Ching* contains many clues to the way energy moves, flows, and accumulates. Hidden within the lines of the hexagrams and their arrangement around a compass of orientations are secrets that explain these flows of energy.

Understanding Yin and Yang

The Chinese have long believed that the creative process goes from one extreme to another, manifesting in endless cycles. So the two extremes of fundamental reality can be expressed as motion (Yang) and quiet (Yin). When one reaches its limit, it becomes the other. So from quiet there is motion, and from motion there is quiet.

It is also written that from this cycle of limits stem the Six, and from the six appear the Five, and then from the five come the Ten Thousand Things. This cryptic sentence is simple to understand when we know what the numbers are referring to. The "Six" refers to the subtle levels of universal Yin and Yang energies. There are three categories that define the qualities of Yin. These are great Yin, balanced Yin, and reducing Yin. Similarly Yang energy can also be classified as great Yang, bright Yang, and diminished Yang. The "Five" are the five elements that express the five manifestations of energy. The Chinese term for energy is chi. These five types of chi are fire, earth, metal, water, and wood. They each have a productive, weakening, or destructive relationship with one of the other elements. Each element also has a Yin as well as

Interaction of Yin & Yang

No limits

LI
Reason
Logic

Limits CHI

Yang

Yin

Action CHI
(HEI)

One Universe

Extreme limits

6 Energies

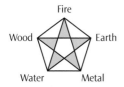

Lesser Yang   Reducing Yin

Bright Yang   Great Yin

Great Yang   Lesser Yin

5 Elements

Fire

Wood   Earth

Water   Metal

8 Trigrams

a Yang aspect. The "Ten Thousand Things" encompass all the things that make up the material and physical world. The forces of Yin and Yang express the manifest universe from voidness or ultimate nothingness to the material ten thousand things. One becomes two. Motion becomes quiet. Yang becomes Yin and vice versa. This creative process of the universe is illustrated here in sequential order. This is the fundamental origin of how the trigrams and then the hexagrams were discovered.

Yang is described as the vibration, pulse, and movement of the universe – energy rotating, moving, and vibrating at different rates. All of this motion takes place against a background of varying manifestations of Yin. Yin is silence, stillness, non-movement, and quiet. The key to understanding Yin and Yang is to realize that one cannot exist to the exclusion of the other, and that one gives rise to the understanding and manifestation of the other. Yin and Yang are interdependent concepts relative to each other. There is simply no Yang without Yin, and no Yin without Yang. Both must be present, otherwise there is nothing. If you remember this concept alone, you will know about balance, your practice of feng shui will be considerably improved, and your interpretation of the five elements and their symbolic meanings will be incredibly enhanced.

When you understand the concept of Yin and Yang you will understand the theory of relativity and its aggregates. It then becomes easier to understand that everything in the universe exists as interdependent aggregates. Nothing exists of its own accord. When there are no aggregates, things simply cease to exist. Everything exists in relation to something else. It is impossible to completely obliterate either Yin or Yang since this will simply cause both to become nothing.

Yin is said to be denser, less energetic, and more material. Yang is lighter, more energetic, and less dense. In the interplay of Yin and Yang, there are a zillion manifestations and variations. The two forces are primordial and everything on earth is an expression of this interaction between the two forces. Despite this, however, earth is regarded as all Yin and heaven is regarded as all Yang. But the things in heaven are regarded as both Yin and Yang when compared to each other. It is the same with all the things of the earth which can be either Yin or Yang and yet when compared with heaven, things of the earth are all Yin.

The correct appreciation of these two supposedly opposing forces is what gives practitioners of feng shui, Taoism, martial arts and other esoteric practices the real potential to make progress in their practice.

In feng shui a genuine understanding of Yin and Yang forces within any environment is often sufficient to cause good levels of energy to be created. It is the same with the practice of Taoist meditation and in the practice of difficult physical exercises that raise the fire of inner chi. When one understands how Yin and Yang energy flows within the human body one becomes exceedingly healthy. And when one understands their flows in the environment one can arrange things to enjoy exceptional good fortune. Meditation based on a good appreciation of Yin and Yang also creates fertile ground for perfect understanding to grow (referred to as divine realizations by religious meditators).

Yin and Yang cosmology also suggests that idea precedes manifest reality. Nothing exists without it first having been conceived in the mind. So the idea of motion precedes actual motion – just as the idea of quiet precedes actual quiet. The idea comes from the mind, so it is mind that moves energy. It is the mind that makes all things happen. Energy moves the body and galvanizes it into action. Energy is the manifestation of the intangible forces of the world and this can have either a Yin or a Yang aspect. At a practical level, the appreciation of Yin and Yang begins with the ability to know what is Yin and what is Yang, and then from that to appreciate what is deemed to be perfect balance between the two. Identification at the gross levels is not difficult. This refers to knowing that sunlight, bright colors, noise, motion, action, heat, dynamism, and so forth are manifestations of Yang, and moonlight, stillness, darkness, cold, death, quiet, and so on are manifestations of Yin.

What is more difficult to ascertain are the subtle levels of Yin and Yang, or knowing the precise moment when Yin transforms into Yang and vice versa. It is also rather difficult to know when perfect balance of the whole has been achieved. Getting the balance right is something that comes with experience and plenty of practice.

Trigrams and hexagrams

The evolution of trigrams and hexagrams is illustrated on the following page. As can be seen, trigrams are symbolic representations of how Yin and Yang interact and, in the process, manifest in varying densities of energy. These become the four images of old and young Yang, and old and young Yin. By adding a Yin and Yang line above these images the eight trigrams are created. These eight trigrams are then combined with each other to make up the 64 hexagrams. So both feng shui and the *I Ching* originate from the two energies that make up the universe – Yin and Yang. When you understand this, you will understand the heart of feng shui.

Hexagrams are six-lined symbols that contain surface and veiled meanings that are not immediately obvious. At first reading, these appear terse and abrupt, but sagely wisdom lies just beneath the surface of the words. The *I Ching's* hexagrams are each made up of two trigrams, one placed above the other. How trigrams evolved into hexagrams is illustrated in the circular expressions of Yin and Yang shown in the hexagram map on page 15.

Trigrams each possess a number equivalent and when these numbers add up to an auspicious combination then the direction indicated by the hexagram is deemed to be auspicious. But in feng shui, the hexagrams of the *I Ching* that appear on the Luo Pan generally apply to Yin dwellings rather than to Yang houses. Thus when you see hexagrams or two rings of trigrams appearing in a Luo Pan these have been put there to condense the codes for undertaking the feng shui of Yin dwellings i.e. grave sites.

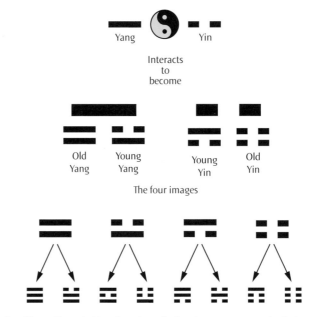

Yang   Yin

Interacts
to
become

Old   Young   Young   Old
Yang   Yang   Yin   Yin

The four images

By adding a Yin and a Yang line above the four images we create the 8 trigrams

Trigram
CHIEN

Trigram
LI

Trigram
KAN

Trigram
KUN

Yang	Yin	Yin	Yang	Yin	Yang	Yang	Yin
Trigram CHIEN	Trigram TUI	Trigram LI	Trigram CHEN	Trigram SUN	Trigram KAN	Trigram KEN	Trigram KUN

Trigrams, on the other hand, are extremely significant in understanding and interpreting the feng shui of Yang dwellings. Each of the eight trigrams suggests a different symbolism, and their arrangement around the sides of the Pa Kua contain meanings for the specific direction each side represents.

The 64 Hexagrams Map

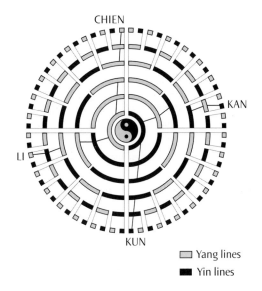

☐ Yang lines
■ Yin lines

6. TRIGRAMS AND THEIR MEANINGS

Feng shui practitioners of the Compass School frequently make extensive references to trigrams. This is because the meanings of the trigrams offer valuable clues as to how to proceed with arranging a space to maximize feng shui. They not only correspond to compass directions, they are also rich with symbolic meanings. As mentioned earlier they represent one of the elements – expressed either as a soft or a dark aspect – and they possess Yin or Yang connotations. They also signify a specific member of the family.

The meanings of the trigrams and their relationship to each other are significant in expanding the scope of feng shui practice. They offer clues as to what can be "activated" and how their symbolism can be interpreted in the physical realm to bring about auspicious outcomes.

The eight trigrams are Chien, the Creative; Kun, the Receptive; Chen, the Arousing; Sun, the Gentle; Tui, the Joyous; Ken, Keeping Still; Kan, the Abysmal; and Li, the Clinging.

Chien

THE TRIGRAM CHIEN, the Creative, comprises three unbroken lines. Its nature is YANG and it is associated with the FATHER, the head of the household, the patriarch, the male paternal. Chien also signifies HEAVEN, the sky, the celestial spheres, strength, activity, power, brightness, bright colors, energy, and perseverance. Chien doubled forms the hexagram of the *I Ching* whose power is to be interpreted in a dual sense i.e. in terms of the strong creative action of the Deity of the Universe and in terms of the creative action of rulers or leaders in the world of mankind. The element associated with Chien is big METAL, and its symbolic animal is the HORSE – denoting power, endurance, firmness, and strength. Additional symbols of the Creative include jade, which is itself the symbol of purity and firmness; round and circular objects; cold and ice. Its compass direction is South in the Early Heaven arrangement of the Pa Kua, and NORTHWEST in the Later Heaven arrangement. In Yang feng shui, the direction of Chien is also northwest, and its number is 6.

Kun

THE TRIGRAM KUN, the Receptive, is made up of three broken lines. The broken lines represent the dark, yielding, receptive, primal power of YIN. The attributes of this trigram are associated with the MOTHER, the female; maternal and devoted. Its image is the whole EARTH, which knows no partiality. The animal symbolizing Kun is the COW with a calf, thereby symbolizing fertility. Kun is the perfect complement of Chien, the Creative (complement and not opposite because the Receptive does not combat the Creative but rather completes it). Kun signifies NATURE, in contrast to spirit, earth in contrast to heaven, space against time, the female maternal as against the male paternal.

In the interpretations of Kun in respect of the destiny of mankind, and when applied to human affairs, the relationship between Chien and Kun refers not only to the man-woman relationship but also to that of the prince and minister, father and son, employer and employee.

According to the *I Ching's* commentary, Kun the Receptive must be activated and led by Chien the Creative if it is to maximize its benevolent essence. The corresponding compass direction of Kun is north in the Early Heaven arrangement, but in Yang feng shui and the Later Heaven arrangement it is the SOUTHWEST which represents Kun. Its element is EARTH and its number is 2.

Chen

THE TRIGRAM CHEN, the Arousing, is made up of two broken Yin lines above an unbroken Yang line. The trigram represents the ELDEST SON and is often associated with movement and decision-making, vehemence and shock. It is symbolized by the DRAGON, which, rising out from the depths, soars magnificently up into the stormy skies. This is represented by a single strong line pushing upward below the two yielding lines. This trigram is represented by a dark yellow color, spreading outwards, which suggests the luxuriant growth of spring that covers the earth with a garment of plants. In the *I Ching*, the doubling of this trigram forms the hexagram Chen, which is described as "... shock, arousing fear, which in turn makes one cautious, and caution brings good fortune ... a symbol of inner calm in the midst of the storm of outer movement."

Chen also signifies thunder, "the kind which terrifies for miles around, a symbol of a mighty ruler who knows how to make himself respected yet is careful and exact in the smallest detail." Chen is placed northeast in the Early Heaven arrangement and east in the Later Heaven sequence. In Yang feng shui we therefore use EAST as the direction that signifies Chen. Its element is big WOOD and its number is 3.

Sun

THE TRIGRAM SUN, the Gentle, is formed by two unbroken Yang lines above a broken Yin line. This trigram represents the ELDEST DAUGHTER and its attribute is summed up in the word "penetrating." The gentle is small wood, it is the wind, it is indecision.

The COCKEREL, whose voice pierces the still morning air, symbolizes it. Among men, it means those with broad foreheads, those with much white in their eyes; it means those close to making gains, so that in the market they get threefold value. Sun is sometimes interpreted as a sign of vehemence. Sun also represents white and whiteness, which is sometimes regarded as the color of the Yin principle and sometimes as the Yang. Here Yin is in the lowest place at the beginning. Sun is placed southwest in the Early Heaven arrangement and southeast in the Later Heaven arrangement. So in Yang feng shui we use SOUTHEAST to represent Sun. Its element is small WOOD and its number is 4.

Tui

THE TRIGRAM TUI, the Joyous, comprises one broken Yin line above two unbroken Yang lines. The two Yang lines are considered the rulers of the trigram, although they are incapable of acting as governing rulers. Tui represents joy, happiness, and the YOUNGEST DAUGHTER. Tui is the LAKE, which rejoices and refreshes all living things. Furthermore Tui is the mouth; when human beings give joy to one another through their feelings, it is manifested by the mouth. A Yin line above two Yang lines illustrates how the two principles give joy to each other and are manifested outwardly. Tui also means dropping off and bursting open. It is the concubine, an association derived from the youngest daughter connections. It is the sheep, which is outwardly weak and inwardly stubborn, as suggested by the form of the trigram. In the Early Heaven arrangement, the trigram is placed southeast, but in the Later Heaven arrangement it is placed WEST, so this is the direction which is used to signify Tui in the application of formulas for Yang dwellings. Its element is small METAL and its number is 7.

Ken

THE TRIGRAM KEN, Keeping Still, comprises an unbroken Yang line above two broken Yin lines. Ken represents the YOUNGEST SON in the family. The trigram literally means standing stiff, a situation exemplified by the image of the mountain. Ken is the MOUNTAIN, a symbol of mysterious significance. Here, in the deep hidden stillness, the end of everything is joined to make a new beginning. Death and life, dying and resurrection – these are thoughts awakened by the transition from an old year to a new year. Ken thus signifies a time of solitude that is also the link between an ending and a beginning.

The element signified by Ken is small EARTH. Under the Early Heaven arrangement of the trigrams, it is placed in the northwest. Under the Later Heaven arrangement Ken is northeast, so in Yang feng shui Ken is represented by the NORHTEAST. Its element is small EARTH and its number is 8.

Kan

THE TRIGRAM KAN, the Abysmal, is made up of one unbroken Yang line sandwiched between two broken Yin lines. Kan represents the MIDDLE SON. It is symbolized by WINTER. Kan signifies pearls, craftiness, and hidden things. It is also considered as a symbol of danger and melancholia because one (strong) Yang line is hemmed in by two (weak) Yin lines. Kan is often referred to as the trigram which suggests toil. Unlike the other trigrams, Kan represents work. It is not a happy trigram.

The symbolic color of Kan is red to resemble the fluid of the body – blood. Kan was originally placed west in the Early Heaven arrangement, but was moved to the north under the Later Heaven arrangement. Thus in Yang-dwelling feng shui, Kan is signified by the direction NORTH. Its element is WATER and its number is 1.

Li

THE TRIGRAM LI, the Clinging, is made up of one broken Yin line hemmed in by two strong Yang lines. Li is LIGHTNING, and represents the MIDDLE DAUGHTER. Li is also represented by the sun, brightness, heat, and dryness. The character of the trigram suggests something firm on the outside but hollow, weak, and yielding within. This trigram strongly implies dependence, but the kind of dependence which is positive and nourishing – as when the plant "clings" to the soil and grows or when "the sun and the moon attain their brightness by clinging to heaven." The yielding element in Li is the central line, hence its image is of a strong yet docile type of cow.

Its element is FIRE and as fire flames upwards, the phrase "that which is bright rises" applies to Li. In the spiritual or divination sense, the brightness of this trigram offers the potential (if the illumination of the brightness stays consistent) for its light to "illuminate" the world. Li occupies the east in the Early Heaven arrangement, but under the Later Heaven arrangement it is in the south, which represents the summer sun that illuminates all earthly things. So in applying the formulas for Yang dwellings we use SOUTH as the direction of Li. Its number is 9.

7. THE TWO TRIGRAM ARRANGEMENTS

The eight trigrams are the root symbols of the *I Ching's* 64 hexagrams. Each trigram is a combination of three straight lines that are either broken or unbroken – much like dots and dashes in a binary code. Trigrams collectively symbolize a trinity of world principles recognized as the subject (man), the object having form (earth), and the content (heaven). The bottom line is earth, the middle is man, and the top line is heaven.

A significant feature of the trigrams is that they transform, and in doing so create new aspects. This is why we have two arrangements of the trigrams – the Early Heaven and the Later Heaven arrangement thus producing two Pa Kuas – the Yin and Yang Pa Kua. In the Early Heaven arrangement the transformations are expressed as "Heaven and Earth determining the directions" – signified by Chien and Kun; "Mountain and Lake uniting" (Ken and Tui); "Thunder and Wind arousing each other" (Chen and Sun); and as "Water and Fire (Kan and Li) not combating" each other. This summary of the trigram relationships reflects their arrangement in the Early Heaven Pa Kua. These descriptions feature in the application of Yin feng shui of grave sites.

In the Later Heaven arrangement, the trigrams express a seasonal cyclical relationship so that their place in the Pa Kua changes. For feng shui purposes it is very significant to note how these trigrams change locations/directions. This movement of places suggest implications on the luck on houses as a result of the way waters (i.e. rivers) flow towards the house/building from one direction and exit in another direction. The same interpretation can also be analyzed with regard to roads that are in the vicinity of your home. Generally when water or roads flow towards the home from an Early Heaven direction (EHD) and flow out in a Later Heaven direction (LHD), the water reflects luck coming from heaven flowing to earth and is auspicious for Yang houses. Moving in the other direction is not auspicious and suggests illness, death, and loss. So note the following summary of the EHD and LHD of the directions based on the trigram transformations of the two Pa Kuas. When roads or rivers near your home flow in the following way they are said to be auspicious for the home.

- *The trigram Chien moves from south (in the Early Heaven arrangement) to the northwest (in the Later Heaven arrangement), so when roads or rivers come towards the home from the south and move away in a northwesterly direction the road is auspicious and benefits the father of the household.*

- *The trigram Kun moves from north to the southwest, so roads or rivers moving towards the home from the north and away in a southwesterly direction are auspicious and benefit the mother of the household.*

- *The trigram Chen moves from northeast to east so roads or rivers moving towards the home from the northeast and away in a easterly direction are auspicious and benefit the eldest son in the household.*

- *The trigram Sun moves from southwest to southeast so roads or rivers moving towards the home from the southwest and away in a southeasterly direction are auspicious and benefit the eldest daughter of the household.*

- *The trigram Tui moves from southeast to west so roads or rivers moving towards the home from the southeast and away in a westerly direction are auspicious and benefit the youngest daughter of the household.*

- *The trigram Ken moves from northwest to northeast so roads or rivers moving towards the home from the northwest and away in a northeasterly direction are auspicious and benefit the youngest son in the household.*

- *The trigram Kan moves from west to north so roads or rivers moving towards the home from the west and away in a northerly direction are auspicious and benefit the middle son of the household.*

- *The trigram Li moves from east to south so roads or rivers moving towards the home from the east and away in a southerly direction are auspicious and benefit the middle daughter in the household.*

8. THE YIN AND YANG PA KUA

The Yin Pa Kua is based on the arrangement of the trigrams around it in accordance with the Early Heaven sequence. In this arrangement, the eight trigrams are named in a sequence of pairs. The Early Heaven sequence is also known as the Primal Arrangement. It was designed by the original founder Fu Hsi, and under this arrangement the two most important trigrams, Chien and Kun – which are the creative and the receptive, heaven and the earth – are in the south and north compass points respectively. Chien is totally Yang and Kun is totally Yin and in the Early Heaven arrangement they form the north-south axis of any given space.

Then follows the Ken and Tui axis i.e. the mountain and the lake. Their forces are interrelated, in that the wind blows from the mountain to the lake while clouds and mists rise from the lake to the mountain. The relationship suggested is thus circular. The Ken-Tui axis is represented by the directions northwest and southeast in this Yin arrangement.

The third axis is formed by Chen and Sun i.e. thunder and wind, which strengthen each other. This is positioned in the northeast and southwest.

Primal Arrangement

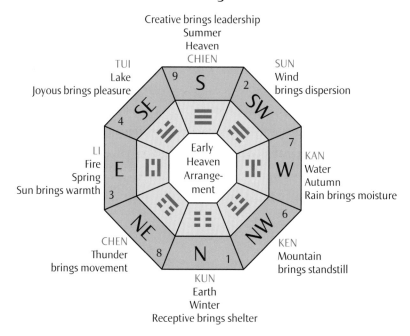

The trigrams Li and Kan, which are fire and water, make up the concluding axis. Though these two elements appear at first to be irreconcilable opposites in the physical world, according to Fu Hsi, in their Primal or "original" state they balance each other so that there is in reality no conflict between them. It is vital to understand this special relationship between the two most destructive and also most powerful elements. While they appear to clash, these two elements also have the potential to harness great power. In the Early Heaven sequence, fire and water occupy east and west respectively and their equivalent numbers here – 3 and 7 – add up to the most auspicious 10. So the Early Heaven relationship between these two elements suggests some powerful force within. Note the sum of 10 prevails in all the four pairs of trigrams suggesting an inner strength to the combinations.

It is further suggested that when the trigrams begin to move and intermingle, a double movement takes place: first the usual clockwise movement which is cumulative and expanding forward, moving and ascending, so that as time progresses this forward movement determines the events which come to pass; second, there is also an opposite backward motion, which folds and contracts, even as time passes, thereby creating "seeds" for the future. The explanation is that if the essence of this backward movement is understood, then the future unfolds clearly.

This is the basis for the Yin Pa Kua arrangement of trigrams, which is concerned with the placement and orientation of tombs to ensure success for descendants.

The Primal arrangement also expresses the forces of nature in terms of "pairs of opposites." Thus thunder, an electrically-charged force, has wind as its opposite. Rain, which moistens the seeds and enables them to germinate, has the sun, which supplies warmth, as its opposite. This example further demonstrates the contention that "water and fire do not combat each other." In comprehending opposite moving forces, consider the trigram Ken, Keeping Still, whose situation describes the termination of any extra expansion and growth. Its "opposite," the Joyous, brings forth "the harvest." Consider also the directing forces of the Creative and the Receptive, which together represent the great laws of existence; these two also comprise a pairing of opposites.

The above expositions of the Primal arrangement seem to suggest ascending and descending forces. Understanding these forces supposedly reveals the "secrets of the future" because the Primal arrangement is supposed to express heaven's view of existence. Such understanding, however, was frequently beyond the modest faculties of most people.

The Later Heaven arrangement

Fortunately, after Fu Hsi came King Wen, who re-formulated the sequence of the trigrams to offer an "inner world" view of mankind that takes a less profound view of the trigrams. Thus came about the Later Heaven arrangement of the trigrams, which bears closer resemblance to the worldly aspects, aspirations, and relationships of mankind.

In the Later Heaven arrangement of the trigrams – also known as the Inner World arrangement – the trigrams are taken out of their groupings in pairs of opposites and are placed instead in a circular temporal progression of their manifestations in the physical realm. Under the new arrangement the cardinal points and the seasons are related. There is a clear perception of cycles, and seasonal, monthly, and daily influences. The arrangement of the trigrams around the Pa Kua was thus drastically altered.

The description of the Later Heaven arrangement of the trigrams in the Yang Pa Kua shows the creative activity of God in the trigram Chen, the Arousing, which stands in the east and

Inner World Arrangement

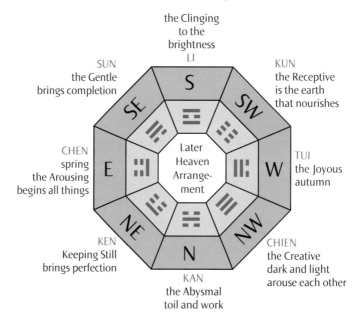

signifies Spring (the beginning). All living things come forth in the sign of the Arousing. They come to completion in the sign of the Gentle (Sun), which stands in the southeast. Completion means that all creatures become pure and perfect. The Clinging (Li) is the brightness in which all creatures perceive one another. It is the trigram of the south. Thus the sages turn to the south (i.e. to the light) whenever they listen to the meaning of the universe. Next comes the Receptive, which means the earth. The earth ensures that all creatures are nourished. Tui, or Joyous, comes in mid-autumn, followed by Chien the Creative in the northwest, and Kan the Abysmal in the north. In the sign of the Abysmal all creatures work. Lastly comes the sign of Ken, Keeping Still, in the northeast where the beginning and the end find completion. Thus the cycle ends.

The sequence of the trigrams also reflects harmony and balance in the year. What is narrated in the above description is the cycle of seasons, the cycle of nature. Trigrams are allotted to the seasons and to points of the compass to reflect the harmony of nature.

One can also extend the annual cycle to that of an ordinary day, so for instance the trigram Chen, while signifying spring, is also representative of morning, the start of the day. The next trigram, Sun, represents the wind, which melts the ice of winter, and wood, which germinates and grows. This takes us to Li, midsummer or noon time. And so on ... The remaining trigrams show the way round the cycle, all the while stressing harmony and balance. The Later Heaven arrangement of the Yang Pa Kua is more easily understood than the early Yin version. It is also more applicable to Yang houses as its basic premise reflects life in the earth realm. In view of this, all latter-day practices of Chinese feng shui use this sequential representation of the Pa Kua to unlock the meanings of the Luo Pan's compass directions when analyzing the chi of Yang dwellings.

The Chinese calendar system of Heavenly Stems and Earthly Branches also relates to the Later Heaven arrangement of the Pa Kua, as do much of Compass feng shui's formulas. For this reason, all feng shui Luo Pans contain this arrangement of the trigrams in one of its inner rings.

9. THE FIVE ELEMENTS AND THEIR CYCLES

The theory of the five elements is a major foundation stone of Compass feng shui. In Chinese this is known as Wu Xing, which conveniently translates as five elements. However, it actually means more: the word wu means five but the word xing is a way of saying "five types of chi dominating at different times." This has been shortened to the word "elements" which seems to have become conventionally accepted into the language of Chinese feng shui and divinition. The five elements are water, wood, fire, earth, and metal.

Water dominates in winter, wood in spring, fire in summer, and metal in autumn. The intersection between two seasons, the transitional period, is dominated by earth. The names of the elements refer to substances whose properties resemble the respective element and help us understand the different properties of the five types of chi.

The properties of the five types of chi are summarized as follows:

Water runs downwards. Water always signifies wealth and success related with money but there is always a danger of overflow. The element of water can therefore bring enormous wealth luck or it can cause great misfortune. Water is a powerful element that cuts both ways. In the Compass formulas water is extremely important and special attention must be paid to it if you want extra income or to improve your monetary lifestyle. Water thus is always symbolic of a money flow. The key is to get the direction of money flow correct!

Wood grows upwards and is an excellent representation of life and growth – so wood always suggests growth and expansion. Think of a seed growing into a tall and luxuriant tree, filled with blossoms and flowers. The chi of wood is pushing upwards. So if success and expansion is what you need and want, look at the best ways to activate the wood element. For this reason a luxuriant growth of plants in the east and southeast is always beneficial.

Fire spreads in all directions. It is radiant and hot, and needs to be controlled. Fire has the potential to suddenly become so big and hot that it can get out of control. Fire brings fame, recognition, and luminosity, the kind of success that can become a double-edged sword; the kind of success that can also burn itself out. Think of it brightening the sky with its flashing red and yellow, but also make sure it keeps burning. Make sure the fire is controlled.

Fire, like water, is powerful and is a double-edged sword. It can be so hot that it burns chi to ashes. Fire is for success, recognition, and popularity.

Metal pierces inwards, is sharp and pointing. It can be deadly and powerful but metal is also the easiest element to control. This is because as an element it is deemed to be unbending and true to type. Metal does not surprise anyone. It is a cold type of chi which, when properly harnessed, brings enormous power. So metal chi stands for power and authority. The danger with metal lies in its unbending nature. The metal element, when energized, can be relentless in its strength. Always have fire energy ready nearby to ensure that metal is always under your control.

Earth The chi of the earth is very warm and embracing. It nurtures and nourishes. Earth energy is protective energy – it embraces and takes care of the home when it is properly energized and balanced. Of the five elements earth is the friendliest and also the most important to have. The earth element must be steady and strong and then the essence of good fortune is present.

Earth is also representative of the center of any home so do remember the importance of this element. At the same time, however, one must also realize that the earth element has a darker side – for instance when it appears as a result of flying star numbers that bring illness, loss, and accidents – and then it becomes dangerous.

In terms of attributes, the five elements are also associated with seasons, directions, numbers, and so forth. The following table gives a quick summary of the different things indicated by each element.

	WOOD	WATER	FIRE	METAL	EARTH
SEASON	spring	winter	summer	autumn	between
DIRECTION	east/SE	north	south	west/NW	SW/NE
COLOR	green	black	red	white	ocher
SHAPE	rectangle	wavy	triangular	round	square
ENERGY	outwards	descending	upwards	inwards	sideways
NUMBERS	3, 4	1	9	6, 7	2, 5, 8
BODY	liver	kidneys	eyes	lungs	stomach

The five elements hold the key to unlocking the meanings of the different plates of the Luo Pan. In addition to the elements allotted to each of the eight cardinal and primary directions, each of the 24 mountain directions in the different plates also has a different set of elements. All the elements assigned to the directions are used to analyze the quality of chi under the different methods of feng shui. In Eight Mansions and Flying Star feng shui, as you will see later, knowing the elements well is a great help in interpreting natal charts and knowing how to cure, how to activate, and how to energize.

Feng shui analysis requires total familiarity with the five elements. But even more important is an understanding of the three cycles of relationships between the elements. There are two primary cycles of interaction that govern the relationship of the elements – these are cycles of either production or destruction. When any two elements are in a productive cycle they give rise to harmony, and when they are in a destructive cycle they give rise to disharmony. The productive cycle is where wood produces fire, fire produces earth, earth produces metal, metal produces water, and water produces wood, and then the cycle starts all over again. The destructive cycle is when water destroys fire, fire destroys metal, metal destroys wood, wood destroys earth, earth destroys water, and the cycle starts again.

The third cycle is the exhaustive cycle. In this cycle basically the productive cycle reverts backwards. Thus fire exhausts wood, earth exhausts fire, metal exhausts earth, water exhaust metal, wood exhausts water, and the cycle starts again. It is this cycle of the five elements that is so useful for designing powerful cures to overcome the afflictions of space caused by the intangible forces of bad flying stars or afflicted directions.

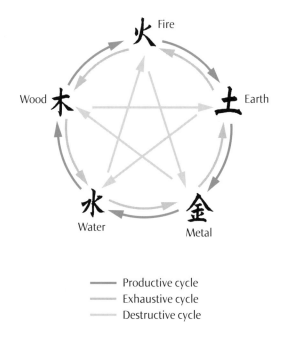

Productive cycle
Exhaustive cycle
Destructive cycle

The cycles of the five element relationships are shown in the illustration above.

To apply element enhancement to your rooms, first commit to memory the element categorization of shapes, seasons, numbers, directions, objects, and so forth. Then, at the most elementary level of the practice, systematically identify the elements in each corner of your home, and move them around to achieve harmony by making sure no conflict of elements occurs in any corner of your home. Instead try introducing symbolic and element enhancers that strengthens the chi of every corner. This is a dimension of Symbolic feng shui practice using the compass.

Some examples of element enhancement:

1 *Refrain from having too much water in the south because water destroys the fire element of the south. However, when the flying stars indicate it is auspicious to place water here you can do so because the water will then be energizing special water energy here. Nevertheless the water feature should never be so big as to overwhelm and conquer the fire completely. Otherwise wealth will be attained at the price of your good name.*

Secrets of the Luo Pan

2   Try not to place round extensions, semi-circular windows, or anything circular in the east or southeast part of your home. This is because round is the shape that symbolizes metal and metal destroys the wood element of the east. Instead, the east is best activated by the presence of water. A lily pond filled with live guppies is an excellent way to bring out the best of the chi of this corner. This is because water produces wood and is thus good for the east.

3   In the north it is an excellent idea to have round and circular structures as the element of this shape is entirely harmonious with this corner of the home. Round is metal, which produces water. What is bad, however, are earth element objects like stones, pebbles, and boulders. It is definitely not a good idea to build a Zen garden made predominantly of stone objects in the north part of the home.

4   In the west or northwest, which are metal corners, placing earth element objects is extremely auspicious. Thus stone sculptures, stone pathways, crystal decorative trees, and natural crystal geodes are auspicious. Avoid fire element objects like bright lights and excessive amounts of red in these corners.

5   In the southwest and northeast use objects that belong to the fire element. These will activate and strengthen the chi here – anything red is gloriously auspicious, bright chandelier lights are also excellent, as are crystals.

10. THE LO SHU SQUARE AND HO TU NUMBERS

In attempting to unlock the secrets of the compass, ancient and latter-day scholars have focused attention on the mysterious Lo Shu magic square of nine numbers.

It is believed that around the year 2205 BC a noble tortoise emerged from the legendary Lo river, carrying on its huge back nine numbers arranged in a grid pattern. The Lo Shu square of numbers had the number five in the center, with the rest of the numbers distributed around the grid as shown in the illustration here. Learning this pattern of numbers is very important in understanding feng shui. It is what gives the greatest potency to feng shui's many formulas. This is because this Lo Shu arrangement of numbers contains the secret key to unlocking countless ways of using directions to manipulate the chi of the environment. This is done through the interpretation of flying star natal charts.

The Lo Shu Numbers

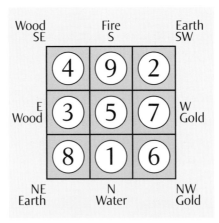

The numbers of the Lo Shu are arranged in such a way that adding them up in whatever direction along any three points in a straight line (whether horizontally, vertically, or diagonally) gives a total of 15. This coincides with the number of days in each of the 24 phases of the solar year. The Lo Shu sequence of numbers is crucial to unlocking the auspicious and inauspicious days of the Almanac. It is also the Lo Shu numbers of the Chinese Hsia calendar which enable those who know how, to calculate good and bad days for undertaking a variety of life rituals – getting married, celebrating birthdays, launching projects, and so forth.

Feng shui masters also came to realize that the Lo Shu numbers held the secrets to understanding time feng shui as it applied to space. Thus the Lo Shu numbers and their sequence of movement around the grids of the square became the basis of formulating the flying star natal chart. In fact the flying star natal chart is expressed in exactly the same way as the Lo Shu chart (see diagram above). How the numbers are placed as stars in a series of natal charts makes up the formula of Flying Star feng shui.

All the most crucial aspects of this formula are condensed into the flying star rings of the Luo Pan. Knowing how to use flying star enables anyone to unlock all the most potent secrets of the Luo Pan. The pattern of numbers of the Lo Shu is thus irretrievably connected with the trigrams of the Later Heaven Pa Kua. We shall be looking at the many permutations and transformations of the Lo Shu numbers throughout the course of this book.

The Ho Tu numbers

The Lo Shu was by no means the first pattern of significant numbers. Chinese myths claim that around 2943 BC Fu Hsi himself received a formation of numbers which, according to legend, was brought to him on the back of a dragon horse that emerged out of the Yellow river. These particular numbers, referred to as the Ho Tu pattern of numbers, (shown in the diagram here) was arranged such that all the odd numbers (except five) added up to 20, as did all the even numbers. More significant in the Ho Tu combination is the way the numbers have been combined: 1 with 6, 3 with 8, 2 with 7, and 4 with 9. Notice that these combinations are pairs of Yin and Yang, odd and even, male and female numbers. All odd numbers are Yang and male while all even numbers are Yin and female.

When they occur the Ho Tu combinations indicate very auspicious circumstances. Thus later on, when you see them as combinations in the flying star natal charts, learn to recognize them because they indicate good fortune. I will reveal how to find out if your house has any of these combinations of numbers when we look at Flying Star feng shui. Also, when you start to compute your Kua numbers under the Eight Mansions of east/west directions, take note that couples who have Kua numbers that reflect the Ho Tu combinations are likely to have a brilliant and happy marriage.

The combination of 1 and 6 signifies wealth as it is placed in the north, which is water. The number 1 prevails here as it is a Yang number. The number 6 is metal which produces water. When this combination is present in your flying star chart activate it with a water feature such as a water lily bowl or a fish pond.

The Ho Tu Numbers

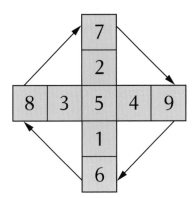

The combination of 8 and 3 signifies wood and is placed in the east. Here the number 3 prevails as it is wood. Combined with earth, wood prevails. In the period of eight this combination is most auspicious as it means growth and expansion. If you have this combination in your natal chart activate it with a healthy, lush plant.

The combination of 7 and 2 signifies fire and it is placed in the south. Here the elements combined are earth and metal thereby creating earth. This combination is brilliant when it is near mountains so if you see it in your natal chart create a mountain with stones and crystals in the part of the home that has this combination.

The combination of 4 and 9 signifies metal or gold. It is placed in the west. Here the combination is of wood and fire, which produces the element of fire. But the element here is gold. This indicates a pairing between two people who become famous and powerful. If this combination appears in the natal chart activate with lots of activity and residents will enjoy extremely powerful success luck.

The mystical attributes of the Lo Shu grid have occupied religious and philosophical scholars through the ages and it survives today as an acknowledged mystery, still potent, and still guarding it secrets. In reality, however, the Ho Tu is more mysterious and one reason it is not more famous is probably because the Ho Tu numbers are applied more in Yin feng shui and only rarely in Yang feng shui – except in advanced interpretations of flying star natal charts.

11. SUPPLEMENTING WITH A MODERN COMPASS

The Luo Pan contains a great deal of information and a great many secrets but, as I have already said, it is not necessary to have one to practice Compass feng shui on a DIY basis. All that is needed is the information contained in the Luo Pan (which is what this book is all about) and an ordinary western-style compass. The Luo Pan is first and foremost a compass for measuring directions, so as long as we use a reliable compass that gives accurate readings of directions, that is all that is needed to utilize the information and formulas of the Luo Pan. I know for a fact that many bona fide feng shui masters supplement their Luo Pan readings with those taken from a western-style compass.

The western compass is similar to any Luo Pan in that it divides directions into 360 degrees around a point of reference. This is divided into eight main directions which are further divided into 24 sub-directions. These coincide with the 24 mountains of the Luo Pan. Each "mountain" measures an angle of 15 degrees (360 divided by 24 equals 15). The three sub-directions of any direction are referred to as 1, 2, and 3 – for instance, the south direction would be divided up into south 1, south 2, and south 3. There are Chinese names for these directions but it is easier to use S1, S2, and S3 to define the sub-directions of south. The other directions are treated in exactly the same way. What you need the compass for is to find out which of the 24 mountains, or sub-directions, is your home's facing direction. You can get this simply by reading the exact degrees off your compass.

Once you have discovered this, it is simple enough to undertake analysis of the feng shui of your home based on that direction and using the methods and techniques in this book. Never estimate directions based on where you think the sun rises or sets. This sort of short-cut feng shui practice is very inaccurate and will not yield good results. Consider the compass as an integral part of your feng shui practice.

The 24 mountains of the compass that are of greatest relevance in terms of practicing Flying Star and Eight Mansions feng shui are the 24 mountains of the earth plate (this is illustrated in the diagram shown on the next page). Note the degrees of demarcation carefully. You can ignore the Chinese words and use N1, N2, and N3 and so on as the names of the mountains. This is how I identify them. However, I also learn the anglicized names of the mountains as this gives me clues to other applications of the 24 mountain directions. I suggest you take it step by step. First learn the names of the 24 mountains according to their compass sub-directions. In the next chapter you will learn how to differentiate between each of the sub-directions of these 24 mountains to fine-tune your practice.

It is a good idea to look for a western-style compass where the sub-divisions of the main directions have already been clearly marked out. This makes it extremely easy to add extra mileage to your little tool. Most feng shui shops should have such a compass. The 24 sub-directions as shown in the following diagram are the 24 mountains of the earth plate and they feature in many of the more popular feng shui formulas. Knowing how to measure these sub-directions correctly and accurately is the first step to practicing Compass feng shui. So do invest in a reliable personal compass. Look for one with the degrees clearly marked around the

24 Mountains of the Compass

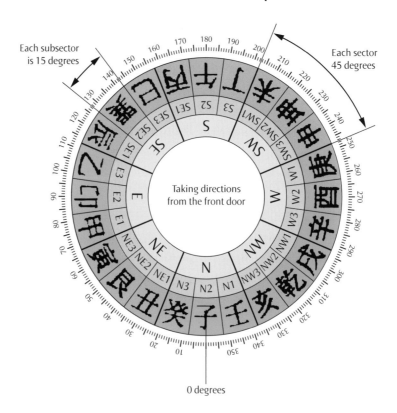

Each subsector is 15 degrees

Each sector 45 degrees

Taking directions from the front door

0 degrees

edge of the compass. Those made with an accompanying ruler are very useful in ensuring that you place the compass square to the door whose direction you are measuring.

12. PRACTICAL NOTES ON TAKING DIRECTIONS

1. GET TO KNOW YOUR COMPASS You will be measuring many different directions as you progress in your knowledge of Compass feng shui so it is useful to know your compass well. Whatever type of compass you use it is useful to note that every compass is different. Familiarize yourself thoroughly with the basics of your personal compass – whether it is a Luo Pan or a modern compass. Learn to read the 360 degrees of directions on your compass so you can instantly get the directions of any place.

2. KNOW THE BASICS ABOUT COMPASS DIRECTIONS There are 360 degrees around a compass. Each of the four cardinal and four secondary directions occupies an angle of 45 degrees. When we extend out the space from any single point occupied by any of the eight directions, the space we are referring to is the space contained within a 45-degree angle. This is best seen when we view each of the directions as a slice taken from a round pie. This is the pie chart method of identifying space within compass directions. The main directions are north, south, east, and west. The secondary directions are northeast, northwest, southeast, and southwest. Each of these eight directions can be divided into three sub-divisions. Thus each 45 degree angle can be subdivided into three subdivisions of 15 degrees each. These three sub-divisions of each of the eight slices of the pie make up the 24 mountains.

3. DIRECTIONS MUST ALWAYS BE READ FROM A COMPASS Please note that while the illustrations in this and all my feng shui books show the direction south at the top of any compass, this does not mean that south is on top when you are identifying the directions of your home. You need the compass to find out where south is in your home. At the same time please note that in Chinese Compass School feng shui, we never use the door or the entrance to determine where south is. You need the compass to point it out to you! It is the same with all the other directions and sub-directions. Those of you who follow other methods of determining the directions of your home please note that you are using another method of feng shui. There is no need to be confused. You will need the compass to determine directions if you wish to apply the secrets of the Luo Pan to your home or office.

4. DIRECTIONS ARE RELATIVE AND NOT ABSOLUTE You must understand how orientations work. Always remember that orientations are always expressed as bearing certain number of degrees from a point. All directions are relative. They are never absolute. What is west to you is east to the house next door. So the point of reference must always be identified first.

5. ALWAYS HOLD THE COMPASS CORRECTLY Always take directions holding the compass perfectly flat on your palm as this ensures an accurate reading. Use a wall as a reference support if you need to and use a compass which has a ruler to ensure it is square to the direction you are taking.

6. TAKE NOTE OF METAL AND ELECTRONICS NEARBY Always make allowances for your compass being affected by metallic or electrical energy fields nearby. It is a good idea to take directions from at least three reference points, then use the average of the three readings.

Some feng shui masters take their compass readings a short distance from the door outside the house so that their compasses are not influenced by any metallic energy near the door. Others even go so far as to take the relevant directions of a building from as far away outside as possible so that their compasses are not affected by any intangible metallic energy around. These two precautions may work for some people although my view is that this also causes the readings to be inaccurate – especially if there are high tension wires and other structures outside that generate electronic signals. These affect the compass readings as well. And in places of high seismic activity, compass readings are affected by underground signals. Use the method that is most comfortable to you and if you need to adapt and adjust for your particular localized situation by all means do so. The intention is to get accurate compass readings.

7. TAKE DIRECTIONS AT WAIST LEVEL This usually yields a better reading of the way cosmic chi flows into your home and into the rooms of your home. When taking compass readings of newly constructed houses note that contractors usually take readings on the floor. There can be a variation of as much as 10 to 15 degrees between a reading taken at ground level and one taken three feet above the ground.

8. ORIENTATIONS You need to know the orientation of your home. Generally this refers to the direction which your main door faces, but sometimes the main door's facing direction is not the same as the general orientation of the house. In such situations use your compass and take all the directions your house can conceivably be facing. You should then refer to the relevant sections of this book for further pointers to help you judge which direction to use. If you are assessing the feng shui of apartments or offices inside multi-level buildings, then you must take a reading of the facing direction of the building itself – it is this direction that is used for casting a feng shui natal chart of the building.

9. DEFINE THE SPACE YOU WISH TO ESTABLISH DIRECTIONS FOR This can be the facing direction of the whole house, or it can be the compass corners of the house. To identify the corners of the interiors it is best to stand inside – preferably in the center of the house if this is possible. It can also be the compass corners of a single room. In this case you should stand in the center of the room and once you have a bearing from there it is easy enough to demarcate its different sectors for further application of formulas.

Note that since the flow of chi is measured within a microcosm as well as taken within the context of the entire macrocosm of space, we need to define what we are examining. In feng shui language this is referred to as the "big tai chi" – i.e. the bigger surrounding space – and the "small tai chi" – which can mean the space of the entire home, the space of the entire apartment building, the space of the individual whole apartment, or it can also mean the space of individual rooms. The same natal chart can be applied to either the big or the small space. Understanding this concept of big and small tai chi is one of the best ways of understanding how to apply the recommendations given in the texts. What you cannot do for the whole house for instance, you may be able to do inside a single room. So if you wish to activate say the northwest corner of the house but cannot do so because there is a toilet there, you can instead activate the northwest of the living room.

10. LOCALIZED ACCURACY IS VERY IMPORTANT Note that localized accuracy of compass reading is a significant factor in correct applications. You need to ensure your readings are accurate, so learn to align the compass for the whole apartment or home, and then repeat it in each of the individual rooms. It should not come as a surprise that every room will show some small variations in the readings of directions. In such cases go with the localized reading since this gives you the correct energy directions of the particular space being investigated. Not all feng shui masters agree on this point so think it through and see if it makes logical sense to you.

11. WHEN THE DIFFERENCE IN DIRECTION EXCEEDS 15 DEGREES If this happens as you move from room to room, it usually indicates some severe imbalance of the energy within the home. This is often a clue that the furniture arrangement and the placement of decorative items is out of sync with the natural flow of energy in the living space. It is then advisable to make some changes to the placement and arrangement of room furniture. One simple and effective method to get the balance right is to move furniture around until the variation in readings falls below 5 degrees. Note that many variable factors can affect the compass reading but metallic and electronic objects have the most impact.

13. DETERMINING THE FACING DIRECTION – VARIOUS CRITERIA

Now that you know how to read the compass correctly and accurately, it is useful to clarify some of the points that will crop up in the course of analyzing the feng shui of your home. One confusing issue facing the novice practitioner is how to determine the correct orientation of a home. Exactly which direction should we take if we are to determine the facing direction of a home? Deciding on the facing direction of a building is very important since this is an essential factor in the casting of a building's flying star natal chart. Any mistake made at this stage causes your entire feng shui analysis to be wrong.

It is easy enough to determine the direction of a building when it is a perfect regular shape and the main door faces the same direction as the general orientation of the building itself. However, when the building is an irregular shape, or is made up of multiple modules, or when there are several entrances with the door facing one direction and the building or home oriented to another direction – this is when judgments have to be made.

This practical difficulty of implementation is made more confusing by the fact that different masters recommend different approaches. My view is that the decision on a building's facing direction depends as much on the visual structure of the building as on its surrounding physical environment. So when there is doubt about a building's facing direction, one should really walk around the building and take note of surrounding roads, views, buildings, and empty spaces.

Here are three different choices which you can use as guidelines to aid you in making a judgment. Consider these guidelines first before thinking through additional factors:

1 *Let the direction indicated by the main door be the facing direction. This means stand at the largest entrance door of the building or house and then, looking out, determine the direction that the door faces. This is one direction that can qualify as the facing direction.*
2 *Let the direction that is facing the main road outside be the facing direction. This is the source of maximum Yang energy. So if the house or building is oriented towards a road even if the door faces another direction take this as the facing orientation of the house.*
3 *Let the direction of the door that is the most frequently used by the members of the family define the facing direction. This is because one definition of main door is that it is the most frequently used door – this is said to be where the mouth of the house is. Based on this criteria this can rightly be regarded as the facing orientation.*

The decision on which of the three interpretations is appropriate must be based on site investigation. All three are feasible alternatives and have serious respectability. I personally know of very successful feng shui master practitioners who use all three options. There is, in

House with Uncertain Facing Direction

Unobstructed view
is here

Main door is here

addition, another viewpoint regarding facing direction and this is the Taoist feng shui view which insists that the facing direction is that which faces the most open space, the most unobstructed view. Thus if your house is built with wide windows or verandahs facing a panoramic view, then even if the main door is located elsewhere and is facing another direction it is the direction of the panoramic view that must be counted as the facing direction of the home. If you use this criterion, problems arise when the house has three sides facing unobstructed views.

Considering all these viewpoints is useful as it makes us think seriously about practicing feng shui in the context of today's modern environment. My advice is to use your own judgment after duly considering each of the above arguments.

All feng shui masters, however, do agree that homes or buildings that have a clearly defined main door have the best potential for enjoying continuous good fortune. Homes that lack this have an uncertain and unstable flow of chi, thereby creating uncertain luck. In the same way, homes or buildings that have competing main doors also cause confusion and instability for the energy entering into the home.

14. SITTING AND FACING DIRECTIONS

Compass feng shui clearly differentiates between facing and sitting directions. These are direct translations of directional bearings to describe the orientation of a house or building. Thus the facing direction is the direction which the front of the building faces. Usually this is also the direction the main door faces but as we have seen in the preceding section there is a certain amount of controversy as to how exactly the facing direction is determined in houses of a non-standard design.

Determining the facing direction correctly is important not only because the flying star natal charts of buildings are based on its facing direction but also because the sitting direction of a building is also derived from its facing direction. The sitting direction is said to be the direct opposite direction to the facing direction. So, for instance, when a building faces north it is said to be sitting south, and when a building faces east it is said be sitting west. This rule holds true all through the 360 degrees of the compass. So if you look at the 24 mountains chart you will note that when a building is facing say the direction of SW2 then it will be sitting in the opposite direction, which will be NE2.

The sitting direction of the building is also referred to as its back direction. In flying star this is said to be its mountain direction, while the facing direction is said to be its water direction. The

Facing and Sitting Directions

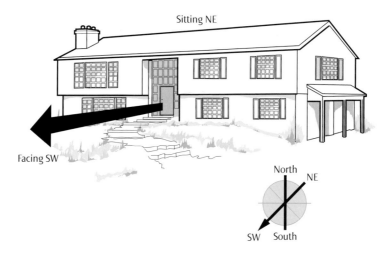

sitting direction of a house is used when one wishes to determine the trigram of the house. This is one of the easiest ways of checking what type of house it is based on its sitting direction. This is a simplified branch of Flying Star feng shui. Thus a Tui trigram house is a house that sits west and faces east. A Tui house favors the youngest daughter or all the young girls of the house. A Chien house is a house that sits northwest and faces southeast. A Chien house is especially suitable for the man of the house, the patriarch.

Later in the book you will see that this formula of trigram houses is an easy and fast method of checking whether a person and his/her house are compatible. Using this method it is also possible to analyze the luck of the house in any time period. Thus month and annual readings of houses can be done using this method based simply on the sitting direction.

15. SUPERIMPOSING THE LO SHU SQUARE ON FLOOR PLANS

Once you know how to take directions and to determine the facing and sitting directions of a building, the next thing is to learn how to superimpose the Lo Shu grid over a floor plan. This is easy to do when the layout of the home or building is a perfect square, with room sizes generally following the sectors of the Lo Shu.

Unfortunately this is seldom the case. Most homes have irregular floor plans and a very personalized layout. Modern homes are rarely, if ever, perfectly square or rectangular. Most also have irregular-sized rooms. There will be missing corners and protruding corners, and sometimes shapes are so irregular even the chi that enters gets confused by the flow created by the shape of the home. So decisions need to be made on whether to include portions of the home that seem to stick out as protruding corners, whether to include garages, patios, and outside verandahs, and how to take account of circular shapes.

There are many variations of house plans and shapes so that superimposing the nine-sector grid can be quite a challenge to any feng shui practitioner – even those who are very experienced. Here are specific guidelines based on my experience, and advice given to me by practicing feng shui masters.

1. SUPERIMPOSE THE LO SHU ON ALL SPACE UNDER A ROOF For interiors in both houses and apartments, the Lo Shu grid should be superimposed over all the built-up area that shares

a roof mass. This means that for apartments it is necessary to superimpose the Lo Shu grid over the whole apartment building to obtain an overview of the chi distribution of the building, before the same Lo Shu square is superimposed on the apartment unit itself. This gives a very accurate assessment of the apartment's overall feng shui and its suitability for its residents, based on their birth date information as well as the natal chart of the building. For houses, all the floor areas covered by the same roof should be included in the area to be analyzed and feng shuied, even if this causes missing corners.

2. MULTI LEVELS SHOULD BE TREATED SEPARATELY When there is more than one level in the building, each level is best treated separately since different floors have different floor areas, different dimensions, and a different layout of rooms. When the different levels are similar the result of the exercise will yield exactly the same indications as to the luck areas of different corners, but when the floor areas are different, the chi distribution will be different.

3. SUPERIMPOSE TWO LO SHU GRIDS When the floor space is very irregular, some practitioners superimpose individual Lo Shu grids on each room separately, thereby going direct to the small tai chi method of analysis. Personally I prefer to use one big grid and treat areas that are empty as missing corners before superimposing the Lo Shu over each separate room.

4. LENGTHEN AND BROADEN LO SHU GRIDS When a floor plan is narrow and long or broad and shallow, some practitioners look at the way the rooms in the home have been arranged and use a six-sector Lo Shu instead of the traditional nine-sector grid. This means dropping the center part of the grid. Personally I continue to superimpose the nine-sector Lo Shu, with the demarcated sectors equally worked out in terms of floor area. The Lo Shu square can therefore, in effect, be stretched vertically or horizontally depending on the dimensions of the space being investigated.

Demarcation according to the Lo Shu square

Superimposing the Lo Shu over a floor plan as shown opposite is a practical method of demarcating sectors within the home. This enables the practitioner to identify the different sectors of the home for purposes of applying the different flying stars and period stars. These "stars" come in the form of numbers, and with the numbers placed inside the grids we can see immediately which numbers are in which room. Here, for instance, the entrance has an auspicious combination of stars. This example shows a house that is facing north and sitting south. So this is a Li trigram house. Its flying star chart shown as the grid of numbers is based on this being a Period 7 house, so the big number in the center of the square is 7. All the other numbers around the grid represent the natal chart of this house.

To fully understand the meanings of the natal chart you must learn the meanings of the individual numbers as well as the combinations of the numbers. The numbers affecting all the different rooms in the house are then investigated. This is the crux of flying star analysis using the secrets of the Lo Pan. For the meanings of these numbers please refer to pages 100–108, 122–126, and 142–146.

The diagram here illustrates how the Lo Shu grid is an especially helpful technique for applying flying star charts to analyze the intangible forces of chi for houses or buildings. It

Lo Shu Demarcations

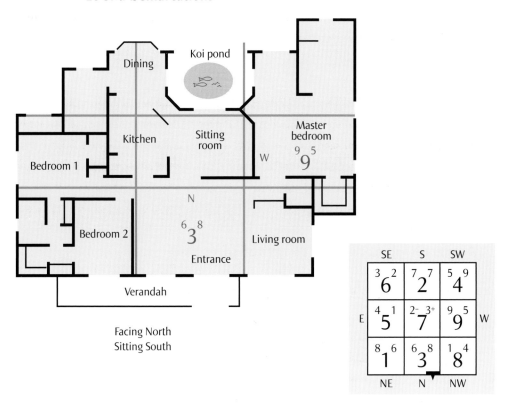

enables you to identify which rooms are auspicious – based on the numbers of the grid there – and which are not, which are best suited for each of the residents, and which rooms need to be enhanced, or require some feng shui cures. This school of feng shui is very fascinating because the results come very fast. One gets hooked on Flying Star feng shui pretty quickly, but take it slowly and go one step at a time. There will be many questions that suggest themselves but they will all have been answered by the time you finish this book.

Pie chart method of demarcation

There is a second method of undertaking the analysis of the interiors of houses, apartments, and buildings. I call it the Pie Chart method. In contrast to the square grid, this method marks out the space emanating outwards from a center point – it superimposes the circular compass itself on to floor plans. This method still requires the flying star natal chart of numbers nearby so that analysis can be made of the spaces demarcated by the circular compass. You will see from the diagram opposite that while the analysis can yield pretty much the same result, the method of defining the spaces is somewhat different. Sometimes, however, certain rooms may fall into different sectors under different methods – then it becomes a matter of judgment as to which method of demarcation you use.

The difference between the Lo Shu method and the pie chart method is the way in which the floor space is demarcated. One method uses compass angles, the other is based on grids. Which part of the house falls into which compass sector can differ according to which method is being used. Again, it is up to you, the practitioner, to decide how you wish to proceed. Use the technique you are most comfortable with.

Demarcation according to layout of rooms

There is a third approach to demarcating the distribution of chi. Under this method, the analysis of flying star natal charts yields drastically different results from the first two methods of demarcation – even when using exactly the same chart. I know of at least three very experienced feng shui masters who are practicing feng shui on three different continents who use the actual layout of rooms on each floor of the house or building to superimpose the natal chart. Their rationale is that chi flows and accumulates according to the physical structures it

Using Compass Demarcations

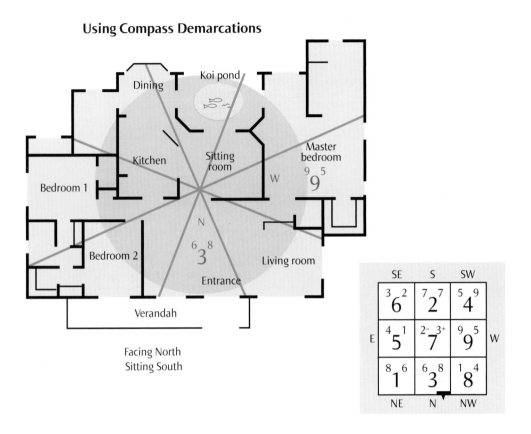

Facing North
Sitting South

confronts. Thus while the flying star natal chart expresses the distribution of chi in any building on the basis of the nine equal-sized sectors within a grid, they contend that in real life the flow and accumulation of chi is neither equal nor static. As a result they allocate the flying star numbers of each of the nine sectors of the grid according to the actual rooms inside the home. Each room (no matter how small or large) literally traps the set of numbers in each of the flying star sectors. Thus storerooms and bathrooms trap one set of numbers while the living room traps another.

This point is best illustrated by an example, so on the following page is the same house shown above but this time the star numbers are allocated according to the physical divisions of the rooms inside the house itself. Note that the master bedroom now has the southwest sector of flying star numbers with the 5/9 combination, while the very dangerous 9/5 is now trapped inside the closet storeroom! Note also that the combinations of numbers for the living room is now 1 and 4 with a base star of 8 where before it was the 6/8 combination.

Demarcations According to Room Layout

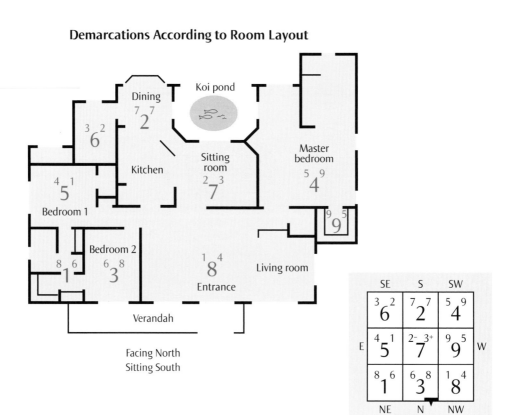

Facing North
Sitting South

When you compare the three methods of demarcating space and superimposing the grid of flying star numbers you will begin to appreciate that at some point you, as the practitioner, will have to make some decisions. You must decide which method is most persuasive and seems the most logical way to apply these ancient formulas. In ancient China most houses – even the Forbidden City itself – were a regular shape and had regular-sized rooms. This made them easier to demarcate for purposes of using flying star natal charts, and superimposing compass sectors and Lo Shu squares. In the context of modern buildings and homes, the practice of advanced feng shui is open to interpretation.

In some cases, where homes are either shallow or narrow, the center grids are dropped altogether. For instance, if yours is a terraced town house, which tends to be deep but narrow, the center vertical grid of numbers is deemed to be missing and only the numbers on both sides are analyzed. This application is illustrated here. Thus the Lo Shu grid is superimposed in a way which ignores the middle set of numbers. The implication, in this case, is that this house cannot benefit from the double 7 in the south sector nor the 6/8 in the north.

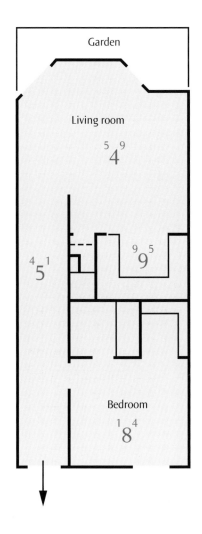

Garden

Living room

5 9
4

4 1
5

9 5
9

Bedroom

1 4
8

	SE	S	SW	
	3 2 **6**	7 7 **2**	5 9 **4**	
E	4 1 **5**	2- 3+ **7**	9 5 **9**	W
	8 6 **1**	6 8 **3**	1 4 **8**	
	NE	N	NW	

Sitting South
Facing North

One way of checking if this method is accurate is to see if the residents have been having good or bad luck. I find that this is a good way of testing if the method I am using is accurate or not. Generally, however, I tend to lean towards the third method i.e. using the room layout to fill in the star numbers, simply because it seems to be the most logical. Think in terms of the rooms being containers receiving the chi.

I do recognize, however, that this third method is also the most difficult to implement when one wants to tap auspicious stars. This is because implicit in this method is the need to knock down walls, create new rooms, and so forth. For instance, if one finds that a set of truly auspicious numbers have inadvertently become trapped in a storeroom, it will become necessary to liberate these auspicious stars – and that means demolishing the walls around the room! Using the same analysis, one can also seek to imprison a bad star combination by building a little room around where it appears.

While you reflect on the merits of each of the above methods of application let me say that many old-style classical masters prefer to use the Lo Shu demarcation, while most of the Hong Kong practitioners swear by the compass demarcations. The more modern practitioners, who seem to be in-tune with the need to adjust old techniques to fit modern-day environments, seem to prefer the last method. There is no right or wrong answer. The practice of feng shui is as much an art as a science. Even though the formulas used are based on scientific measurements and calculations, nevertheless, judgment based on experience is still called for.

Personally I have used all three and prefer to make up my mind only after I have been on site. In my own home, however, I have used the third method to successfully trap a set of bad stars. I used the same method to expand the floor area where we have a very auspicious set of stars – by getting rid of all the walls. My suggestion for now is that you reflect upon this as we will be thinking more about it when we reach the chapter on flying star analysis and applications.

PART TWO

The 24 Mountains

16. THE 24 MOUNTAINS OF THE EARTH PLATE

THE 24 MOUNTAIN DIRECTIONS OF THE EARTH PLATE (ALSO KNOWN AS THE MIDDLE PLATE) IS THE BASIC SET OF 24 DIRECTIONS THAT IS MOST FREQUENTLY USED IN MASTER PRACTITIONERS FENG SHUI FOR YANG DWELLINGS. THE EARTH PLATE UNLOCKS MANY SECRETS OF COMPASS FENG SHUI, ESPECIALLY THOSE THAT HAVE TO DO WITH DIFFERENT BRANCHES OF FLYING STAR CHARTS.

Flying Star feng shui teaches the practitioner to cast the feng shui natal chart of any home or building. This chart shows how the numbers move, whether in a Yin mode or a Yang mode, and is based on the Yin and Yang aspects of the 24 mountains of the earth plate. This determines how the numbers are placed into the nine sectors of a flying star natal chart. This chart reveals the nature and distribution of chi within buildings and homes. It is invaluable, not only for identifying auspicious and inauspicious sectors of any building but also for enhancing good fortune and protecting against misfortunes before they have a chance to materialize. This is the great wonder of Flying Star feng shui – when you know how to use it, you will be amazed by what it can and will do for you and your family in all aspects of life.

The north direction of the earth plate refers to magnetic north. So a western-style compass (which uses magnetic north) can be used for the application of Flying Star feng shui. Those of you who have your own Chinese Luo Pan can use it to determine the directions, but any good western-style compass that enables you to identify the three sub-sectors of each of the eight directions will do just fine.

Familiarize yourself with the 24 mountains of the earth plate. Study their elements and their Yin/Yang aspects. Note that the elements of the 24 mountains are not the same under the different plates. In the beginning the three plates can be confusing, but once you develop an easy familiarity with the rings of the Luo Pan, it all becomes clear very fast.

Examine the compass below, which shows the earth plate. This diagram has been included here for your reference. Store it carefully as this provides the knowledge of the Luo Pan translated into English. Note the directions indicated by the "12 animals" (another name for this is the 12 earthly branches). You can see from this compass which direction corresponds to your animal sign. Thus if you are born in the year of the rat then the direction N3, or kway, is good for you. If you were born in the year of the monkey then the direction W1, or ken, is good for you. In this way anyone can immediately correlate their animal sign with a compass direction to see which direction supports them. This is a simple guideline that is very easy to use immediately. When the corner of your home that corresponds to your animal sign is

The Earth Plate

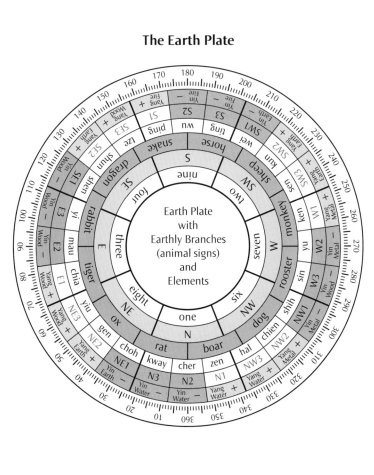

afflicted because it is occupied by the toilet, or is wasted because a storeroom is there, then you should try to do something about it. Change the usage of the room and bring in Yang chi (with lights, music, or activity) to make the space work for you.

Spend some time familiarizing yourself with this simple compass, particularly the anglicized names of the 24 mountains and their directional equivalents. Meanwhile, to understand the rings of this simplified compass of the earth plate, turn your attention to the illustration below. This clearly illustrates what each ring stands for.

Having focused on the 24 mountains – their names as well as their directions – look at what the element of each of the 24 mountains is. These elements have either a Yin or a Yang aspect. When it is Yin it indicates that the chi here travels in a minus, i.e. backward, mode. When it is Yang it indicates that the chi of this mountain direction travels in a plus, i.e. forward, mode. This is the basis on which flying star chart numbers for the mountain and the water stars (more on this later) move from one grid sector to another – either in a minus (numbers descending) or a plus (numbers ascending) mode as indicated by whether the element is Yin or Yang.

If you examine the whole compass you will discover that there is a correlation between the Yin and Yang of the sub-directions (eg. N1, N2, N3) that make up the 24 mountains and the ring which indicates the Lo Shu numbers. From this correlation we obtain one part of the flying star formula, the part that pertains to the way the numbers of the mountain stars and water stars move from sector to sector. So note the formula on the following page.

The Rings of the Earth Plate

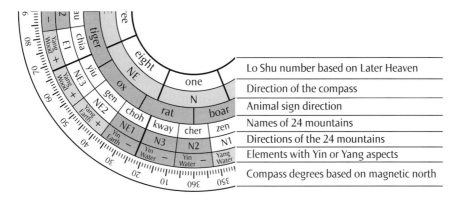

Lo Shu number based on Later Heaven
Direction of the compass
Animal sign direction
Names of 24 mountains
Directions of the 24 mountains
Elements with Yin or Yang aspects
Compass degrees based on magnetic north

Odd numbers (1, 3, 5, 7, and 9) move from sector to sector in a Yang, Yin, Yin mode for the three sub-directions, and this corresponds to plus, minus, minus mode.

Even numbers (2, 4, 6, and 8) move from sector to sector in a Yin, Yang, Yang mode for the three sub-directions and this corresponds to a minus, plus, plus mode.

Later – in the section on how to cast the flying star natal chart – you will learn how to apply this formula to cast the feng shui natal chart of any home or building.

17. EIGHT MANSIONS AND PERSONALIZED DIRECTIONS

I first introduced this formula on personalized auspicious and inauspicious directions based on one's Kua number in my first international book on feng shui (*The Complete Illustrated Guide to Feng Shui*) and I believe it was the sheer potency of this simple yet powerful formula that contributed to so many people getting interested in feng shui. The Kua formula got me hooked on feng shui, and I am certain it has opened many people's hearts and minds to the ancient practice of feng shui.

The Kua formula is based on one's date of birth and gender, and this is all that you need to work out your Kua number. Actually it is the year of birth which is important but because we need to find the lunar year equivalent of the birth year we need the date of birth. Your Kua number will instantly tell you if you are a west- or an east-group person, and will enable you to identify your personal element, your personal trigram, and your lucky number. All these personal attributes enable you to personalize the feng shui of your space, to customize the clothes you wear, and the decorations and symbols you surround yourself with in order to attract amazing good luck. The Eight Mansions, or Kua, formula is a very simple and easy formula to use – a great deal easier than the flying star formula and, I have to say, just as potent. For those of you encountering it for the first time, the Kua formula is condensed in the following graphic. For those who already know it please read on to expand and deepen your knowledge and application of this powerful formula. With knowledge of the 24 mountains you can now go deeper in fine-tuning your use of Eight Mansions.

To adjust for the lunar calendar, you will need to refer to the Chinese lunar calendar to see if your date of birth falls in the previous year. Remember that the lunar New Year starts on a

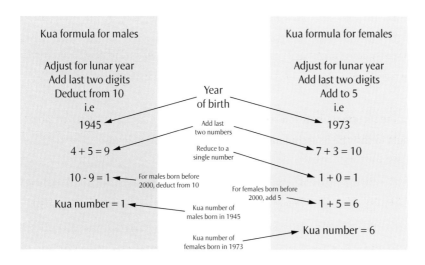

Kua formula for males

Adjust for lunar year
Add last two digits
Deduct from 10
i.e

1945

4 + 5 = 9

10 - 9 = 1

Kua number = 1

Kua formula for females

Adjust for lunar year
Add last two digits
Add to 5
i.e

1973

7 + 3 = 10

1 + 0 = 1

1 + 5 = 6

Kua number = 6

Year
of birth

Add last
two numbers

Reduce to a
single number

For males born before
2000, deduct from 10

For females born before
2000, add 5

Kua number of
males born in 1945

Kua number of
females born in 1973

N.B If you were born in the weeks preceeding the start of the lunar new year (Jan or early Feb), use the last 2 digits of the year **before** your year of birth to calculate your kua

different western date each year – some time in January or February. So you require the Chinese lunar calendar (see appendix) to see if your year of birth needs adjustment. Some masters use the solar calendar where the New Year date is deemed to be 4 February. I prefer to use the Chinese lunar calendar for greater accuracy.

The formula above gives you your Kua number, which can also be regarded as your personal number. From your Kua number you then derive your personal, or self, element and your personal trigram. The table here gives you these two attributes.

KUA	1	2	3	4	5	6	7	8	9
TRIGRAM	Kan	Kun	Chen	Sun	*	Chien	Tui	Ken	Li
ELEMENT	Water	Earth	Wood	Wood	*	Metal	Metal	Earth	Fire

*note: Males with Kua 5 change it to 2, females with Kua 5 change it to 8

The Kua number also assigns to each person four auspicious and four unlucky directions. These are dependent on whether you are an east-group or a west-group person (see the chart below). If you are a west-group person then west-group directions are good for you and east-group directions bring bad luck and loss. If you are an east-group person then east-group directions are good for you and west-group directions bring bad luck.

West-group directions are west, northwest, southwest, and northeast. East-group directions are east, southeast, north, and south

The four good directions are given special names. Sheng chi directions are the best. These are growth directions and if you are able to tap your Sheng chi, it brings success, a smooth life, and plenty of wealth and expansion luck. Your life gets better and better. Nien yen directions bring love, romance, and a good family life. It is also a direction which indicates obedient children. Tien yi directions bring longevity and good health. When you tap this direction you will rarely get sick. Fu wei directions are great for personal growth and development. These four good directions can be energized in various ways. You can actually be very creative in the way you use these directions (my earlier books focused on many applications of your good directions).

The four inauspicious directions begin with Ho hai, the basic bad luck direction. Wu kwei is the five ghost direction, while Lui sha is the six killings direction. The worst direction is the Chueh ming or total loss direction. The idea is to avoid activating any of one's bad directions.

Kua Chart of Personalized Directions

Auspicious directions   Inauspicious directions

Kua	Wealth	Health	Love	Growth	Bad luck	5 Ghost	6 Killing	Total loss	Group	Self element
1	SE	E	S	N	W	NE	NW	SW	East	Water
2	NE	W	NW	SW	E	SE	S	N	West	Earth
3	S	N	SE	E	SW	NW	NE	W	East	Wood
4	N	S	E	SE	NW	SW	W	NE	East	Wood
5	Becomes Kua 2 for males, becomes Kua 8 for females								West	Earth
6	W	NE	SW	NW	SE	E	N	S	West	Metal
7	NW	SW	NE	W	N	S	SE	E	West	Metal
8	SW	NW	W	NE	S	N	E	SE	West	Earth
9	E	SE	N	S	NE	W	SW	NW	East	Fire

Use this chart to look up your good and bad directions. From the chart you can see which of the eight main directions indicate good luck for you and which indicate bad luck.

Going Deeper

Using this book, however, we can go deeper to fine-tune the selection of our auspicious directions. We can use the 24 mountains to tell us how good a good direction and how bad a bad direction can be. The 24 mountains can also reveal whether a bad direction's bad influence has been modified by the influence of the 24 mountains. So when you add the dimension of the sub-directions into your practice of Eight Mansions you can select which of the sub-directions among your good directions is best for you.

Example: if your Kua number is 6 then your Sheng chi, or wealth direction, is said to be west. But you can choose from W1, W2, or W3. To see which of these sub-directions is best for you examine these three sub-directions. On close examination of the 24 mountains you will see that they are either Yin or Yang, and that they correspond to:

1 *The 12 earthly branches i.e. the animal signs. So if you are a rooster then W3 is best, and if you are a monkey then W1 is best. Note that W1 is a Yang direction and so is more suitable for a woman. W3 is a Yin direction and so is more suitable for a man. This creates the balance of Yin and Yang.*
2 *The eight heavenly stems To see which of the stems is good for you, refer to section 20 on the heavenly stems of the 24 mountains.*
3 *The four major trigrams These refer to the father, the mother, the son, and the daughter. One of these trigrams will correspond to your status in your family so when tapping your good direction it is also wise to check if any of these directions also coincide with your good directions.*

When studying the 24 mountains of the earth plate it is therefore useful to investigate them in detail and learn how to apply them to your selection of directions in order to maximize luck and attract wealth, health, and happiness. When none of the sub-directions seem to apply to you in any special way use only the Yin and Yang essence to fine-tune your choice of directions.

18. THE 12 EARTHLY BRANCHES OF THE 24 DIRECTIONS

A key component of the 24 mountains is the set of 12 sub-directions that represent the earthly branches. This is another name for the 12 animal signs under which all of us are born. The animal signs are the earthly branches of the year. Note that under the Chinese Ganxhi system there are two elements in each year. One is the element of the "earthly branch" and the other is the element of the "heavenly stem."

Generally when these two elements of the year are in a harmonious relationship – i.e. when one produces the other as in water with wood, or wood with fire – then the year is said to be a harmonious and auspicious year. When these two elements are in discord – i.e. they are in a destructive relationship with each other – it is said to be an inauspicious indication for the year. For instance in the year 2002, which is a horse year, the element of the earthly branch is fire, but the element of the heavenly stem is water. So the heavenly stem element of water destroys the earthly branch element of fire. The elements of the year 2002 are thus said to indicate discord. This explanation tells you something about earthly branches and heavenly stems, which are used in the metaphysical practices of the Chinese.

In Four Pillars Destiny analysis, for instance, the elements of the stems and branches of one's Four Pillars are charted. These refer to one's year, month, day, and hour of birth. In feng shui, instead of using the four pillars chart to determine our self element, we use the Eight Mansions Kua number. We also use the same formula to determine our good and bad directions. And then we use the 24 mountains chart to go deeper. Of the 24 directions, 12 of them correspond to the 12 earthly branches.

So in addition to Kua directions we now add the extra dimension of earthly branch direction to fine-tune our choice of directions. Therefore from a choice of 45 degrees we now narrow it down to 15 degrees. The earthly branches of the 24 mountains are shown in the graphic illustration opposite.

From the illustration you can see the corresponding compass directions for each of the animal signs. Note also the name of the mountain:

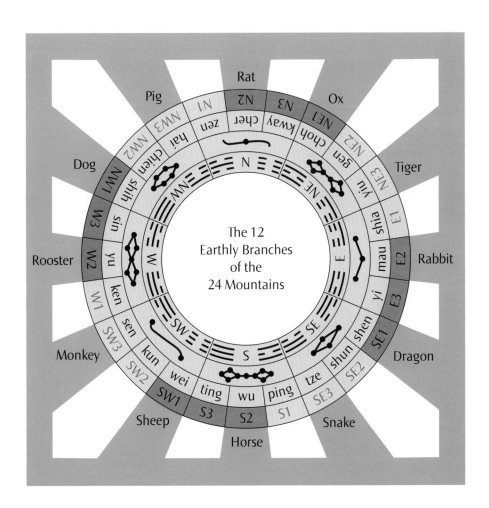

Rat – N2 known as Cher

Ox – NE1 known as Choh

Tiger – NE3 known as Yiu

Rabbit – E2 known as Mau

Dragon – SE1 known as Shen

Snake – SE3 known as Tze

Horse – S2 known as Wu

Sheep – SW1 known as Wei

Monkey – SW3 known as Sen

Rooster – W2 known as Yu

Dog – NW1 - known as Shih

Pig – NW3 - known as Hai

These earthly branch directions are an additional dimension that can be taken into account in an Eight Mansions analysis. So if you are born in the animal sign of the dog you know that NW1 is a good direction for you. If you are a west-group person this mountain direction will be excellent for you. And if you are an east-group person the good indications of the earthly branch harmony of this sub-direction will cancel out any bad luck brought to you by this inauspicious west direction.

At a practical level this means that if you have no choice but to sit facing northwest and it is bad for you based on Eight Mansions, then if you are born in the year of the dog, you can shift your angle slightly to face NW1 and nullify any harmful luck coming towards you. If you were born in a pig year, then NW3 would do the same for you. This is because NW3 is the direction of the earthly branch that corresponds to the pig. This extra dimension of the Eight Mansions formula is extremely useful for those whose choice of sitting, sleeping, and facing directions is limited. It expands the possibilities and the alternatives for the practitioner considerably.

19. THE FOUR IMPORTANT TRIGRAMS OF THE 24 MOUNTAINS

In addition to fine-tuning based on the animal signs, it is also possible to fine-tune based on another set of criteria that is also represented in the 24 mountains. This is done by utilizing the four trigrams that make up the 24 mountains in the secondary directions of northwest, southwest, northeast, and southeast.

Based on the Later Heaven arrangement of the trigrams around the compass, these four directions correspond to the four component members of the family unit. Thus the northwest or, more accurately, the sub-direction NW2, is the place of the trigram Chien which stands for the father. The southwest or, more accurately, the sub-direction SW2, is the place of the trigram Kun which stands for the mother. The northeast or, more accurately, the sub-direction NE2, is the place of the trigram Ken (also spelt Gen) which stands for the youngest son (though in this case it doesn't apply exclusively to the youngest son). The southeast or, more accurately, the sub-direction SE2 is the place of the trigram Shun (or Sun), which stands for the eldest daughter (though in this case it doesn't apply exclusively to the eldest daughter). This is illustrated here.

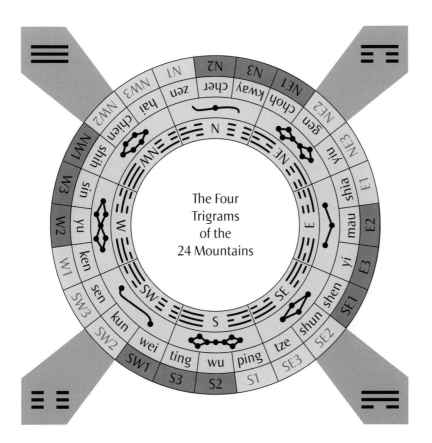

From this diagram you can see that these four sub-directions, or mountains, correspond to a component member of the family unit. Using this knowledge you can fine-tune the choice of auspicious directions according to which member of the family you are. Thus if your Kua number is 8, the southwest direction is good for you, and if you are the mother then SW2 is the direction for you. If you are the father, son, or daughter, taking this direction means whatever good luck comes to you will also benefit your mother.

If your Kua number is 1 and the direction southeast is good for you, then if you are a daughter, sitting facing the sub-direction SE2 will give double benefit. If you are the father, mother, or son of the family then whatever good luck you gain will also benefit the daughter. This part of the formula can only be used when you are considering these four directions.

This piece of information is also useful when a direction is bad for you. Thus if the direction northwest is bad for you because you are an east-group person, but you have no choice but to face northwest in your office, then if you are the father in your family you can choose NW2 of the three sub-directions to nullify any bad effect. What is required is only a very subtle shift in direction and this can easily be done with a compass and a swivel chair. This then is the huge advantage of knowing these fine points of Compass Formula feng shui.

20. THE EIGHT HEAVENLY STEMS OF THE 24 MOUNTAINS

The last component set of directions of the 24 mountains is what is referred to as the Eight Heavenly Stems (in the Chinese calendar system there are really 10 heavenly stems but here only eight of them are represented in the 24 mountains). This is shown in the illustration below.

Note that the heavenly stems are the first and third sub-directions of the four cardinal directions north, south, east, and west.

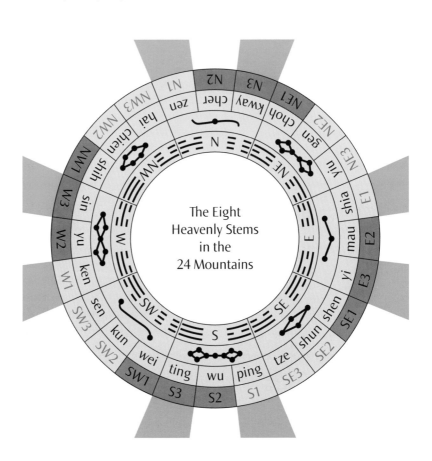

In the north the element is water. The stems here are Yang Zen (N1) and Yin Kway (N3).

In the south the element is fire. The stems are Yang Ping (S1) and Yin Ting (S3).

In the east the element is wood. The stems are Yang Shia (E1) and Yin Yi (E3).

In the west the element is metal. The stems are Yang Ken (W1) and Yin Sin (W3).

To use these directions to fine-tune of your application of the Eight Mansions formula you will need to know the element of the heavenly stem of your year of birth. Once you know that (please check against the calendar at the back of the book) then take note of the elements above but also note if the elements have a Yin or a Yang aspect.

Note the ELEMENT of each of the mountains again

S1	PING is YANG FIRE	S3	TING is YIN FIRE
N1	ZEN is YANG WATER	N3	KWAY is YIN WATER
E1	CHIA is YANG WOOD	E3	YI is YIN WOOD
W1	KEN is YANG METAL	W3	SIN is YIN METAL

Use the productive and destructive cycle of the elements to find out which of the stem directions are good for you and which are bad. The stem direction that has an element that produces your element, is good for you. That which has an element that destroys or exhausts your stem element is bad for you.

Next note that Yang water destroys Yang fire. But Yang water does not destroy Yin fire.

Note also that Yang wood produces Yang fire. But Yin wood does not produce Yang fire.

So how do you determine if you are Yin or Yang? Simple – by your gender. If you are female you are Yin and if you are male you are Yang.

The use of the heavenly stems formula can be confusing and difficult. If you find it is not worthwhile to apply this part of the formula you can pass on it. But facing a stem that brings luck is said to be most auspicious.

21. AXIS DIRECTIONS FOR EAST AND WEST GROUPS

One of the confusing principles of the Kua formula, and one which causes real difficulties on a practical level, arises from the sitting and facing directions recommended by advanced feng shui practice. This advocates two things:

1 *To enjoy benevolent chi and benefit from auspicious luck, west-group people should live in west houses and east-group people should live in east houses. Houses are defined as west houses when they are sitting in a west direction. Houses are deemed to be east houses when they are sitting in an east direction. Note that the sitting direction is the opposite of the facing direction.*

2 *West-group people should have their main door facing a west direction and east-group people should have their main door facing an east direction, preferably their Sheng chi direction since this is the direction that brings success, wealth, and good fortune.*

(Note that the west-group directions are west, northwest, southwest, and northeast, and the east-group directions are east, southeast, north, and south.)

The confusion arises because when your house faces east it is sitting in the direct opposite direction – which is west. The same is true of houses that face northwest (a west direction), they are said to be sitting southeast, an east direction. So, on the face of it, it appears that there can be a contradiction for those whose Sheng chi directions are east, southeast, west, or northwest. It would appear that in using their Sheng chi direction as their house facing direction, it makes their house into the opposite group and that brings bad luck for them.

From this it would seem that those whose Kua numbers define these four directions as their Sheng chi direction simply cannot tap their Sheng chi direction for their main front door. This drawback applies to those with Kua numbers 1, 6, 7, and 9.

If you look at the following diagram very carefully, you will see that the allocation of directions into east or west looks very much like the Yin Yang symbol. Note that among the east directions north stands alone and among the west directions northeast stands alone. This resembles the bit of Yin in Yang and the bit of Yang in Yin (see the little dots in the Yin Yang tai chi symbol in the middle of the Pa Kua). This suggests the directions north and northeast are somehow significant.

East group
South
Southeast
East
North

Kua numbers
1, 3, 4, and 9

West group
Southwest
West
Northwest
Northeast

Kua numbers
2, 5, 6, 7, and 8

The importance of the directions north and northeast lie in their opposite or sitting directions. This introduces the concept of the axis directions. This piece of information is significant in advanced feng shui which goes into deeper detail of formulas. It does not mean that simple feng shui does not work, but when you become more advanced in your practice you have wider choices. It enhances the breadth and scope of your practice. It also enables you to understand some of the principles of Compass formulas a little better.

When you understand the concept of axis directions you will realize that it is possible for west-group people to live in houses that face west and still be deemed to be west houses; and for east-group people to live in houses that face east and still be deemed east houses. This becomes possible when the house is facing an axis direction.

The axis direction for east houses is north/south
The axis direction for west houses is northeast/southwest

You will see that north and northeast are the two stand-alone directions in their group. So north has access to its fellow east-group directions through the opposite direction of south. So when you face north, you will be sitting south and vice versa. Since both are east directions you are facing and sitting east. So basically if you are an east-group person then the north/south axis houses are excellent for you. Similarly, northeast has access to its fellow west-group directions through the opposite direction southwest.

When you face either northeast or southwest you will be facing and sitting west, and if you are a west-group person a house with a northeast/southwest axis is excellent for you. What then about couples who do not belong to the same group. It would seem equitable to have the house face east and sit west (and vice versa) thereby benefiting both. This is not of course the optimum solution since neither party benefits that much. If it is the only way then it can be used as a solution. However, I would prefer to use the axis to benefit the breadwinner of the house and then have another door that is beneficial for the other spouse. This way the benefits are more certain and clear cut.

22. THE SECRET OF THE CASTLE GATE ENTRANCE

There is a little-known gem regarding feng shui directions – the theory of the Castle Gate Entrance. It is said that this was one of the powerful secrets of one of Singapore's most famous feng shui masters of the last century – the monk Venerable Hong Choon. According to this theory, when a building succeeds in tapping the castle gate entrance, residents within the building will prosper through an entire cycle of 60 years.

The castle gate theory requires the entrance of the building to be positioned at an angle of 45 degrees to the main road. If you visit Singapore you will see that a number of high-profile head offices were built this way. Probably the most famous and an often-quoted example of feng shui magic is the way the entrances into the Hyatt Hotel were repositioned to tap this theory. According to feng shui folklore, the feng shui of the Hyatt was designed by the revered and legendary Venerable Hong Choon. It is said that after the master repositioned the door to tap the castle gate theory the hotel's fortunes improved immensely.

In addition it was also believed that the monk added a Yang water feature to make the castle gate even more auspicious. This was not still, or Yin, water. Yang, moving water in the form of fountains were added to strengthen the castle gate feature of the hotel. When the glass door directions (not the whole building's orientation) were changed it was feared the castle gate created was not strong enough, hence the addition of the Yang water feature.

When the castle gate is blocked for some reason, either by a large pillar or tree, the chi in front of the door is said to be negatively disturbed. In such a situation additional Yang energy is needed to pull the chi from outside into the building. Having a revolving door at the castle gate does this. This feature is said to be extremely auspicious when the flying stars at the entrance into the building are also auspicious. The revolving gate activates and churns up the benevolent chi. Note that to cast the flying star chart one takes the facing direction as though the building faces the main road even though it may have been angled at 45 degrees to the main road to tap the castle gate direction. This is a very vital fine point to remember.

To obtain the best possible influence from the castle gate secret it is a good idea to add decorative features that resemble three joss sticks (please note it has to be three, not one or two) just in front of the building. These are said to be offerings to the God of wealth. In Singapore clever Chinese tycoons who believe in feng shui place three round conical-shaped structures in front of their building that resemble giant joss sticks – except that these structures are actually giant flower pots decorated with live orchids and other foliage plants.

Having these features is very different from having three pillars as part of the front of the building. When you have three pillars they are said to keep the mouth of the building perpetually open. Unable to close, the entrance to the building then resembles a mouth that cannot shut – so all the money rolls away! So don't add three stand-alone pillars at the front of the building. They do not represent good feng shui. A popular method of activating the front of the building and strengthening the castle gate door is to place weatherproof statues of the three star Gods Fuk, Luk, and Sau on the roof facing the direction of the house. When I visited Shanghai recently, I took a tour of many of the grand old houses of this wonderful and fast-growing city and discovered several examples of this method of activating the front part of the home.

Finally, please note that a little-known tip given in a feng shui almanac recommends that one of the best directions for the main entrance is one that faces just off the southwest/northeast axis. This is said to be an excellent axis direction for a main entrance that taps the castle gate theory. This is known as the "earth axis." In the texts these directions are described in accordance with their names Wei and Choh.

Wei is actually the mountain direction SW1 while Choh is the mountain direction NE1. This axis direction is doubly auspicious for people who belong to the west group of Kua directions. It is said that at least 90 percent of the buildings in Singapore's prosperous Orchard Road face this axis direction (either SW1 or NE1). If you can tap either of these directions, try also to simulate inward-flowing water as this is one of the best ways of accumulating wealth. Make sure the water flows in, though. When water flows out in full view of the main entrance it signifies complete emptiness or total loss.

23. USING THE MANKIND PLATE TO ANALYZE THE IMPACT OF BUILDINGS

The 24 mountains of the mankind, or man, plate are known as the middle ring 24 mountains. The man plate lies 7.5 degrees to the right of the earth plate and it is said to move slower than the earth plate. North in this plate is not magnetic north, it is Polaris north. And since the star Polaris is part of the constellation, the elements of the 24 mountains in this plate reflect the stars and constellations. Thus the elements of its 24 mountains are different from those in the earth plate.

In feng shui practice, the man plate is excellent for determining the effect and impact of surrounding rock formations. In the old days this formula was used to determine the auspiciousness or hostility of nearby mountains and valleys. In the modern-day environment, however, feng shui masters have very effectively used this same formula to analyze the impact of the buildings, towers, transmission lines, and many other modern structures that surround buildings. Analysis is based entirely on the interaction of elements assigned to the house and to buildings in its vicinity. In terms of practical usage, this formula is excellent for checking how new buildings erected near you will affect the feng shui of your home. This investigation can be undertaken at two levels. You can investigate the effect on the whole house or you can investigate the impact on individual residents.

To determine whether nearby buildings are beneficial to the house and its residents we need to determine:

1   *The sitting direction of the house being analyzed.*
2   *The personal element based on the Kua number of the residents.*
3   *The direction of the nearby building whose feng shui effect we wish to analyze.*

From the directions we can determine the element of the house and of the nearby building based on the man plate. An easy way to determine the directions is to measure the compass direction using an ordinary compass and then deduct 7.5 degrees from the reading. This enables one to determine the sitting direction of the house as well as the direction of the building being investigated.

To determine its effect on the house, we then apply this formula:

1   When the building is in a direction whose element produces the element of the house the building will bring patronage and resource luck to residents of the house.

2   When the building is in a direction whose element is similar to the element of the house the building will bring prosperity to the residents of the house.

3   When the building is in a direction whose element is destroyed by the element of the house the building will result in money and servants for the residents of the house.

4   When the building is in a direction whose element is produced by the element of the house the building will exhaust/deplete the energy of the residents of the house.

5   When the building is in a direction whose element destroys the element of the house the building will cause grave misfortunes to the residents of the house.

A good way to understand this formula is to look at an example.

Example: Let us investigate the effect of three buildings on a house that faces W3 and so is sitting E3. This makes its sitting element earth. Look at the illustration on the next page – what is the effect of the three buildings marked A, B, and C on the fortunes of the house ?

Building A is in front of the house on its right and it is located in the NW2 direction. The element of that direction is wood (marked "wo" in the illustration). Since wood destroys earth, building A will cause misfortune to befall the house. It is therefore necessary to counter the killing chi coming from that building.

The best thing to do is to hang a metal windchime in the NW2 direction – this will intercept the destructive chi coming from that direction (note metal destroys wood). We can also hang red curtains in the NW2 direction, or install a bright light here to simulate fire energy. This will exhaust the killing chi emanating from the building.

Building B, which is behind the house, is in the direction NE3 and from the chart we can see this direction belongs to the water element (marked "wa" in the illustration). Since earth destroys water this building is good for the house as it brings servants and money luck to the home. There is no need to enhance or do anything with regard to this building.

Building C is in the W1 direction, which is of the fire element (marked "fire" in the illustration). Since fire produces earth this building creates excellent prosperity luck for the house. So a clear view of this building would be most beneficial. Indeed if you have a bright

House Facing W3 Sitting E3

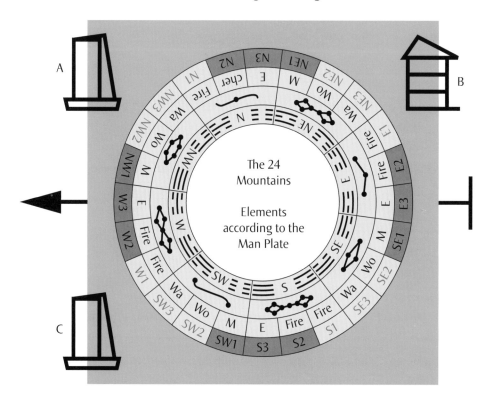

hall – i.e. a small patch of empty space in the W1 direction of your home – this should act as a magnet for the chi created by the building to flow benevolently towards you.

It is also possible to investigate the effect of nearby buildings on the luck of individual residents by looking at the personal element of the resident. This means that while nearby buildings affect the house in general, they also have varying effects on the different residents of the household.

Apply the same formula after you have obtained the personal element based on KUA numbers. For those with Kua numbers 2, 5, or 8 the effect of the buildings will be exactly as analyzed for the house, since the element of these numbers is earth.

Those with Kua 1 – water, will benefit from buildings B and C but building A will be exhausting.

Those with Kua 9 – fire, will benefit from building A and C but building B will cause serious bad luck. To overcome plant trees in that direction.

Those with Kua 3 and 4 – wood, will benefit from building A and B but not building C.

Those with Kua 6 and 7 – metal, will benefit from building A but not buildings B and C.

As an exercise see if you can work out how I arrived at the above conclusions. As an aid in the analysis you might want to refresh your knowledge of the three cycles of the five elements. Knowing how the these five elements interact with each other is the key to this formula.

24. THE HEAVEN PLATE TO ANALYZE THE FLOW OF WATER

The heaven plate moves 7.5 degrees faster than the earth plate and it uses true north – based on the sun dial – as the reference point of its compass directions. The 24 mountains of the heaven plate are usually found in the Sarn He Luo Pan (Three Harmony Luo Pan). It is used for deciphering auspicious incoming and outgoing water flows for Yin dwellings. In the old days the feng shui of grave sites was deemed to be exceedingly important since it is believed that good water flows in the grave sites of one's ancestors had a direct bearing on the wealth of descendants. In modern times Yin feng shui continues to be practiced, especially by wealthy families keen to ensure that their family wealth stays intact or expands. As I prefer to pass on this dimension of feng shui, Yin feng shui does not fall within the scope of this book.

There are portions of the Three Harmony School on water flows that do, however, apply to both Yin and Yang dwellings. Yang dwellings are referred in the texts as "dragons dens." This refers to the water flow principles that must be followed based on the facing directions of houses and buildings.

The Rings of the Heaven Plate

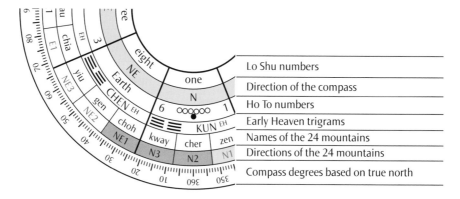

	Lo Shu numbers
	Direction of the compass
	Ho To numbers
	Early Heaven trigrams
	Names of the 24 mountains
	Directions of the 24 mountains
	Compass degrees based on true north

The above illustration is a segment of the 24 mountains of the heaven plate which is usually read in conjunction with the Ho Tu numbers. This is because the Ho Tu numbers feature strongly in the Yin water formulas.

For Yang dwellings, however, what you need to remember is that for directions referring to the heaven plate we must add 7.5 degrees to readings taken from a standard compass. This adjusts it and makes it a heaven plate reading. This way amateur practitioners wishing to use the water flow guidelines contained in the Three Harmony water formulas, which are reproduced here, can do so.

First take the facing direction of the house. Remember that this is usually the same as the facing direction of the main front door – unless the main door is facing a garage, a side road etc. (See section on facing directions.)

For all houses and buildings with the facing direction E1, N1, E2, N2, W1, S1, W2, or S2 the water should flow past the front of the house from left to right i.e. in a clockwise direction. Note that this applies to all houses facing a cardinal direction but the fine-tuning is that the house should not be facing any of the third sub-directions. In such houses the prosperity is Yang prosperity and the source of the wealth comes from the men of the family.

For all houses and buildings with the facing direction NW2, NW3, NE2, NE3, SW2, SW3, SE2, or SE3 water should flow past the front of the house from right to left i.e. in an anti-clockwise direction. Once again note that this applies to all houses facing a secondary direction but the fine-tuning is that the house should not be facing any of the first sub-directions. In houses with this kind of facing direction and this kind of water flow, what flows is Yin prosperity and the source of wealth comes from the women of the family.

The Dragon Gate water flow

In addition to the flow of water past the front of the house, there are also guidelines that govern the flow of water coming into the house and going out of the house. This is known as the Dragon Gate water flow. There are different guidelines for Yin and Yang dwellings, and these are based on the sitting direction of the house. (Please note that the Dragon Gate water flow is different from the Water Dragon formula.)

To create Dragon Gate water it is necessary to determine the sitting direction of the house. (Remember, the sitting direction is the opposite of the facing direction.) From the sitting direction one can then name the house based on its trigram. Please take directions carefully since the formula is based on the 24 mountains and thus refers to segments of only 15 degrees, which means that one has to be more careful to ensure a correct reading. Also remember that all references to the 24 mountains here refer to the heaven plate so adjustments must be made by adding 7.5 degrees to any reading taken with a compass that measures magnetic north. This is because the heaven plate is based on true north.

The Dragon Gate water flow is summarized below.

1 **Chien House** *sitting northwest – water should flow in from the northeast or the south and flow out in an E1 direction. It can also flow out in a southwest or west direction.*

2 **Kan House** *sitting north – water should flow in from the southwest and flow out in an SE2 direction. Water can also flow out in an east or northwest direction.*

3 **Ken House** *sitting northeast – water should flow in from the east or west and flow out in a SW2 direction. Water can also flow out in a north or SE direction.*

4 **Chen House** *sitting east – water should flow in from the south or southwest and flow out in a SW2 direction. Water can also flow out in a north or southeast direction.*

5 **Sun House** *sitting southeast – water should flow in from the west and flow out in a N1 direction. Water can also flow out in a south or northeast direction.*

6 *Li House* sitting south – water should flow in from the northwest and flow out in a NE2 direction. Water can also flow out in a west or the southwest direction.

7 *Kun House* sitting southwest – water should flow in from the south or north and flow out in a NE2 direction. Water can also flow out in a northwest or east direction.

8 *Tui House* sitting west – water should flow in from the north or southeast and flow out in a NE2 direction. Water can also flow out in a northeast or south direction.

In feng shui it is necessary to establish a very clear distinction between the flow of water and the presence of bodies of water. Since water makes up such a vital dimension of feng shui, many of the old texts are devoted exclusively to analyzing the impact of water and water flows on the feng shui of houses. There are, in actual fact, several different ways to approach water feng shui. In the context of modern day situations, unless you own a country estate with big tracts of land, water feng shui is beyond most of us – especially those living in apartments. Thus for the past many years I have focused more on the feng shui of small water features rather than on large water flows. The above formula can be used if you have a small garden and you are able to create a flow of water – perhaps you can use it to design the drains around the home – otherwise, I would suggest that you focus instead on water as it applies to Flying Star feng shui. Using flying star in conjunction with the symbolic principles relating to water, it is possible to create awesome wealth luck without having to worry about the Dragon Gate method.

Time Changes in Feng Shui

PART THREE

25. CYCLES OF TIME PERIODS IN FENG SHUI

PERIOD CYCLES OF TIME

The Upper Period
Reigning number 1 1864 to 1883
Reigning number 2 1884 to 1903
Reigning number 3 1904 to 1923
The Middle Period
Reigning number 4 1924 to 1943
Reigning number 5 1944 to 1963
Reigning number 6 1964 to 1983
The Lower Period
Reigning number 7 1984 to 2003
Reigning number 8 2004 to 2023
Reigning number 9 2024 to 2043

ACCORDING TO CHINESE BELIEF, THERE ARE FENG SHUI CYCLES OF TIME, EACH COMPLETE CYCLE LASTING 180 YEARS. EACH CYCLE IS MADE UP OF THREE PERIODS – THE UPPER, MIDDLE, AND LOWER PERIODS. EACH OF THESE PERIODS COMPRISE 60 YEARS, AND THESE IN TURN ARE MADE UP OF THREE SUB-PERIODS LASTING 20 YEARS EACH. THUS EACH CYCLE OF TIME COMPRISES NINE PERIODS OF 20 YEARS EACH. YOU MAY ASK WHY NINE PERIODS? THIS IS BECAUSE THERE ARE NINE NUMBERS IN THE LO SHU MAGIC SQUARE.

In each of these periods of 20 years, there is a reigning number, from one to nine, which represents the period. This number has a great deal of significance in Compass feng shui. To start with, each 20-year period has its own Period Lo Shu chart, with the reigning number of the period placed in the center. This is referred to as the Period's Base Lo Shu square for purposes of feng shui analysis.

We are presently (at the time of publication) living in the period of seven, although it comes to an end on the 4 February 2004. As we near the end of the period of seven, the star number seven, which was lucky throughout the 20 years of this period (1984–2003), loses its luster and slowly turns weak before eventually becoming very unlucky in the period of eight (2004–2023) which follows.

The Period Lo Shu square

The Period Lo Shu is arrived at by placing the period reigning number in the center of the nine-sector grid. From this, the remaining numbers of the square can be allotted their "place" in the grid. This placement is based on the sequence of numbers in the original Lo Shu square. This sequence is often referred to as the "flight of the stars" and it is this movement of numbers that unlocks the secrets of the flying star natal chart. It is therefore an excellent idea to begin by learning this sequence, since you will meet up with it again when we learn how to cast the natal chart of buildings. For now let us look at three things:

- *The original Lo Shu square, with 5 in the center*
- *The flight of its numbers i.e. where 6, 7, 8 and so on are placed*
- *How we derive a period seven Lo Shu chart with the number 7 in the center*

The ORIGINAL LO SHU SQUARE shown opposite is a nine-sector grid with numbers one to nine placed in the sectors of the grid. Any three numbers vertically, horizontally, or diagonally add up to 15 – the number of days that make up one cycle of a waxing or waning moon. Hence the Lo Shu is the basis of all time-related feng shui formulas. Note the following:

- *the number 5 is in the center*
- *the next number 6 is in the northwest*
- *the number 7 is in the west*
- *the number 8 is in the northeast*
- *the number 9 is in the south ... and so on*
- *the element of each sector of the grid*

Remember the directions, numbers, elements of the grid. When you have become thoroughly familiar with the original Lo Shu square it becomes much easier to understand all other

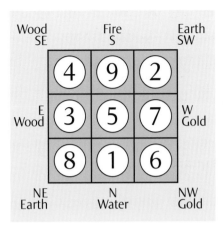

squares that are derived from it. It is important to remember that the numbers and elements associated with each other in this original square continue to hold when we study all the new charts that are created as part of the flying star method of feng shui. For example 9 is always fire, 1 is always water, and so forth. Similarly the base element of the southeast sector is always wood, while northwest is gold, and so forth. Study this original Lo Shu square well – it is the key to the time cycles of feng shui.

THE FLIGHT OF THE NUMBERS shown here indicates the way the numbers move. Starting from the center number 5 notice the next number 6 has moved to the northwest – this is referred to as the flight of the star numbers. The old masters, looking at this flight, realized that

The Flight of the Numbers

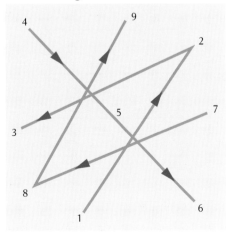

it formed the powerful symbol of the Nine Kings. This is also the sign of the Sigil, which is found in the Hindu as well as Jewish traditions. This sign is believed to be a powerful protective sign, and can be worn as an amulet that protects against premature death.

In Flying Star feng shui this sign is important as an easy way of remembering how the numbers are placed around the nine-sector grid. Follow the directions of the arrows. Note that the numbers here fly in an ascending fashion, getting higher from 5 to 6 to 7 and so forth. Later you will see that these numbers can also fly in a descending order.

PERIOD SEVEN LO SHU SQUARE The square shown below represents the base chart of numbers of the period seven. This is also the base chart of all houses and buildings that were constructed or renovated during the period of seven, that is between 1984 and the end of 2003 (or 4 February 2004 to be exact). This is usually referred to as the period seven chart. Note that the center number is 7, so the next higher number, which is 8, has been placed in the northwest. This follows exactly the same sequence you saw earlier. Similarly all the other numbers from 8 to 9, and then to 1, 2, 3, and so forth are placed in sectors in exactly the same sequential arrangement as the in the original Lo Shu square.

Work this out in your head. Once you know the sequence of how the numbers move you will be able to create your own chart for all the nine periods of the whole cycle of 180 years. All you need is the center number. With this center number all other numbers are placed in the other sectors in exactly the same sequence as in the original Lo Shu.

	SE	S	SW	
	6	2	4	
E	5	7	9	W
	1	3	8	
	NE	N	NW	

	SE	S	SW	
	9	5	7	
E	8	1	3	W
	4	6	2	
	NE	N	NW	

	SE	S	SW	
	1	6	8	
E	9	2	4	W
	5	7	3	
	NE	N	NW	

	SE	S	SW	
	2	7	9	
E	1	3	5	W
	6	8	4	
	NE	N	NW	

	SE	S	SW	
	3	8	1	
E	2	4	6	W
	7	9	5	
	NE	N	NW	

	SE	S	SW	
	5	1	3	
E	4	6	8	W
	9	2	7	
	NE	N	NW	

	SE	S	SW	
	6	2	4	
E	5	7	9	W
	1	3	8	
	NE	N	NW	

	SE	S	SW	
	7	3	5	
E	6	8	1	W
	2	4	9	
	NE	N	NW	

	SE	S	SW	
	8	4	6	
E	7	9	2	W
	3	5	1	
	NE	N	NW	

Study the Lo Shu Period squares of all the periods reproduced here. Follow the sequence in all of them.

These transformations of the Lo Shu square also hold the key to several minor formulas that relate to time sequences in feng shui analysis. The key to each of these Lo Shu squares is the center number. As long as you know the center number you will be able to generate the Lo Shu chart of any period. This holds true also for the year, the month, the day, and even the hour of each day. So the above charts can also double up as annual or monthly charts. All you need is the center number.

Every year, month, day, and hour (known as the Four Pillars) has what is referred to as its Lo Shu number. As long as you know the Lo Shu numbers of the year, the month, the day, and the hour, you can generate the Lo Shu chart for any particular moment in time and form the year, month, day, and hour charts to analyze the distribution of auspicious and killing chi in any given place. The "place" here is always expressed as a compass direction. This is how feng shui masters analyze the feng shui of disastrous world events – through what I call Predictive feng shui.

The reigning numbers of periods seven and eight

Coming back to houses and buildings, you now know that the numbers of the reigning periods enable the practitioner to draw up the base natal charts of buildings, houses, cities, and even countries for feng shui analyses.

The reigning number of every 20 years gives its name to that period. Because the origin of these numbers lie in the mysterious mathematical arrangements of the Lo Shu and is influenced by the Pa Kua, it is widely believed by feng shui masters that this number – the number that "rules" the period – is extremely auspicious during the period. The number seven therefore represents prosperity and wealth creation during the current period. It is regarded as an auspicious and lucky number until the end of the period. If it is incorporated into a car number, a telephone number, a bank account number, a house number, or any other personal number, it is believed to bring good luck. However, as we are now nearing the end of the period of seven the energy and the strength of the seven's auspicious qualities are now weakening.

When you study time dimension feng shui you must take note of this and start to investigate the things that need to be done to protect your feng shui when the change of period occurs on 4 February 2004. When we enter the period of eight the number seven transforms into a total loss number that brings loss, bloodshed, and violence. I have included an entire chapter devoted to what can and should be done to cope with this changeover of period.

For now, however, note that period seven corresponds to the trigram Tui which represents the direction west, the element metal, or gold, a young girl, a lake, the mouth, young children, and most of all, joyousness. Some say the rise of women and the importance of communication during this period (since 1984) are manifestations of period-of-seven attributes. Feng shui practitioners point to the emergence of young women in the professions and in leadership positions. Tui stands for things spiritual, so we are reminded of the popularity of the New Age and other neo-spiritual revivals. Things related to the mouth – singing, speaking, the growth of the media – are all thought to be due to the influence of the period of seven. The popularity of feng shui itself is a manifestation of the period of seven's influence.

In the analysis of the trends of the different periods it is possible to correlate each of the numbers (except the center number 5) with the trigrams of the Pa Kua. This is based on the numbers in the original Lo Shu that are each associated with the trigrams in the Later Heaven Pa Kua. On the basis of this it is possible to describe characteristics that lend themselves to interpretations for the periods. Since the period of seven is coming to a close it is also useful to take a brief look at what is in store for us in the period of eight.

The period of eight begins on 4 February 2004 and it will last for 20 years. The number eight corresponds to the direction northeast, which is represented by the trigram Ken. Its element is earth and it signifies keeping still, like the mountain. Ken personifies the young man and it is associated with the end of everything and a new beginning. In feng shui the number eight, which is a very auspicious white number, represents very near prosperity. Although we are not yet in the period of eight, its auspicious effect is already being felt and those who have the Kua number eight, or whose house number is eight, will benefit significantly as soon as we enter the next period. In terms of numbers the combination of seven with eight signifies great good fortune during the period of seven because it means current as well as future prosperity. However, as soon as we enter the period of eight, these numbers turn soar and weak. We should now be looking at combinations of double digit eights, as well as combinations of eight and nine. These two numbers combine fire and earth and are most auspicious because fire produces earth.

26. THE CHINESE LUNAR AND SOLAR CALENDARS

The Chinese have both a lunar and a solar calendar. The lunar calendar is the calendar the majority of English-speaking Chinese are most familiar with. In this calendar the New Year date changes back and forth between January and February from year to year. It is necessary to check the hundred-year calendar to see the start of each New Year. This is the calendar that is used in the celebration of Chinese New Year, in determining one's animal year of birth, in our investigation of our life's destiny analysis, and in determining the heavenly stem and earthly branch elements of our year of birth. When we use the Kua or Eight Mansions formula we use this lunar calendar. (A 100-year lunar calendar is reproduced at the back of this book for easy reference.)

The solar calendar

Flying star feng shui periods are not based on the lunar calendar, which is the more popular and well-known calendar, but on the solar calendar. This is also known as the Hsia calendar. This calendar differs from the lunar calendar in that it judges 4 February to be the start of the year (there is a margin of error of one day in certain years but 4 February is a safe day to use as the changeover date from year to year). This corresponds to the Lap Chun, or start of spring, in the year.

Flying star annual and monthly periods are based on the solar, or Hsia, calendar, and the Lo Shu numbers of each year and month are expressed on the basis of this calendar. Thus when we speak of flying star annual and month charts it is important to note that our equivalent western calendar dates are based on this calendar. The charts opposite summarize the Lo Shu numbers for the years and months of the solar calendar.

These charts enable anyone to work out the Lo Shu squares of every year and every month, with cut-off dates that enable you to convert to a western calendar. To obtain the Lo Shu chart for any particular year or month, look for its equivalent Lo Shu number. Remember that this is the reigning number that goes to the center of the chart and all other numbers are then filled in, in accordance to the sequential arrangement discussed previously. It is possible to see which number goes in which sector of the grid. For example, in 2003 the annual flying star chart has 6 in the center and looks like this.

	SE	S	SW	
	5	1	3	
E	4	6	8	W
	9	2	7	
	NE	N	NW	

Reigning numbers for solar calendar years 2000 to 2025

YEAR	REIGNING NUMBER	YEAR	REIGNING NUMBER
2000	9	2013	5
2001	8	2014	4
2002	7	2015	3
2003	6	2016	2
2004	5	2017	1
2005	4	2018	9
2006	3	2019	8
2007	2	2020	7
2008	1	2021	6
2009	9	2022	5
2010	8	2023	4
2011	7	2024	3
2012	6	2025	2

Reigning numbers for the solar calendar months in various years

START OF MONTH	YEAR of RAT, RABBIT, HORSE & ROOSTER	YEAR of DOG, DRAGON, OX & SHEEP	YEAR of TIGER, PIG, SNAKE & MONKEY
4 FEB	8	5	2
6 MARCH	7	4	1
5 APRIL	6	3	9
6 MAY	5	2	8
6 JUNE	4	1	7
7 JULY	3	9	6
8 AUGUST	2	8	5
8 SEPTEMBER	1	7	4
8 OCTOBER	9	6	3
7 NOVEMBER	8	5	2
7 DECEMBER	7	4	1
6 JANUARY	6	3	9

82

Note: The dates may have a variation of one day plus or minus. The previous chart is the summary of the 10,000 year calendar which should be consulted for more accurate analysis of the luck according to different months of the years. First check the animal earthly branch ruling in the year, then use the reigning numbers of each month to derive the flying star chart for that month.

27. ANNUAL AND MONTH FENG SHUI CHARTS

Using the table on page 81 anyone will be able to generate the relevant flying star chart for each month of any year. First find out what animal reigns in the year under investigation. Thus 2003 is the year of the sheep. So the Lo Shu reigning number for the first month (starting 4 February and ending 6 March) is the number 5. You will note that the reigning number for year 2003 is 6 so to obtain the annual and month chart for the first month of the year 2003 this is what you do. You combine the annual with the month chart. This is shown below.

From the flying star chart you will see that west sector is very auspicious that month (with 8/7 combination), the southwest residents have a quarrelsome month when there is a tendency to get sick (3/2 combination), and the south sector has the fire star activated by the 9 month star. Once you know all the meanings of the numbers and also how to analyze a natal chart you will be able to undertake analysis for every month for every room of the house. In addition, month and year analysis can also be extended to see how the numbers combine with the chart of the house itself. It is this that makes Flying Star period feng shui so awesome. If you are beginning to get excited by flying star, this is just the beginning. There is more to come.

Year Chart + **Month Chart** = **Flying Star Chart**

SE	S	SW
5	1	3
4	6	8
9	2	7

E ... W (Year Chart)
NE / N / NW

SE	S	SW
4	9	2
3	5	7
8	1	6

E ... W (Month Chart)
NE / N / NW

SE	S	SW
5^4	1^9	3^2
4^3	6^5	8^7
9^8	2^1	7^6

Month 1 year 2003

SE	S	SW
6	2	4
5	7	9
1	3	8
NE	N	NW

E ... W

$+$

SE	S	SW
5	1	3
4	6	8
9	2	7
NE	N	NW

E ... W

$=$

SE	S	SW
6^5	2^1	4^3
5^4	7^6	9^8
1^9	3^2	8^7
NE	N	NW

E ... W

Month 12 year 2002

Let us consider a second example: the annual and month chart for the 12th month of the year 2002 – the year of the horse. You will see that in the year of the horse the reigning number is 7 while that of the 12th month (6 January 2002 to 4 February 2003) is 6. To construct the chart you combine the year and month charts.

Looking at the flying star chart for month 12 in the year 2002 we can see that the northwest room of any house in that month will benefit from the auspicious stars 8 and 7. We also know that residents sleeping in the southwest room of any home will tend to have misunderstandings in their love life or marriage. The illness star 2 has also flown to the north and combines with the annual 3 star there. This indicates a really hard time – illness and quarrels.

From the above two examples you can proceed to create monthly charts to analyze the luck of the different rooms in your home in any period. Once you have created the charts you will need to refer to chapters on number analysis to get a full picture. As well as being used for predictive feng shui, flying star time charts are also used by some advanced practitioners to track the rise and fall of stock markets, of currencies and other indices.

28. ANNUAL AFFLICTIONS AND FENG SHUI CURES

Another dimension of time period feng shui, and one that is vital to the practice as a whole, is the examination of annual afflictions. These afflictions sometimes have the capability to cause tremendous bad luck. Depending on what type of affliction it is, and in which sector the affliction hits, sometimes these annual horrors can cause bankruptcy, loss, and even death. This is one of the greatest motivations behind my passion for feng shui. It is simply so vital to take note of these afflictions. Illness, business collapses, loss of employment, accidents, separations, and divorces can often be attributed to these annual afflictions. Knowing when they might occur will help us prevent them.

Three major annual afflictions

In all there are three major annual afflictions which everyone should take note of. These are:

- *the Five Yellow, also known as Wu Wang*
- *the Three Killings, also known as Saam Saat*
- *the Grand Duke Jupiter, also known as Tai Tsui*

I usually post annual affliction warnings on my websites, together with suggested cures for the year. Those of you reading this book can now work out the afflictions on your own. The important thing is to take note of the cures that you can use to overcome these afflictions – although of course the best cure is to avoid them altogether if possible. When you know that your bedroom is afflicted by either the Wu Wang or the Saam Saat it really is best to move into another room for the year. This is because the cures may reduce the effect but when the affliction is in a sector that strengthens it (or your furniture and interiors have symbols that strengthen it) then whatever cures you place may not be totally effective.

Furthermore, note that when your bedroom or front door is afflicted by any one of these three afflictions and the month and year numbers there are also inauspicious, then the danger is considerably heightened. The best thing then is to move out of that room for the year of the affliction – even if it means sleeping in the living room. If you really cannot do this then all you can do is to try to use a symbolic cure to reduce the impact of the affliction. But it is hard to overcome these afflictions altogether.

The sector that houses the main door is usually most vulnerable to these afflictions. So when any affliction hits the sector where the main door into the house is located, the whole house will feel the effect. In this case it is definitely advisable to use another door for the duration of that year (if possible). This is because the opening and closing of the door activates the affliction.

In the year 2001 the Five Yellow swung into the southwest sector. This is the sector that houses my main door. That new year, however, I was so busy I forgot to install my metal cures. On 4 February every single member of the household fell ill: my mother, my husband, myself, my children, my maid – everyone. Only then did I remember the Five Yellow. I installed metal windchimes immediately and we got better. To ensure no more illness I closed my southwest door permanently for the duration of 2001 – this made certain that the sector would not get activated by the opening and closing of the door. If using an alternative door is not an option for you, then you are left no option but to install special feng shui cures to reduce the effect of these afflictions.

29. WORKING WITH THE GRAND DUKE TAI TSUI

Probably the least worrisome of the three annual afflictions is the Grand Duke Jupiter, who changes location every year. He is regarded by the Chinese as the God of the Year and it is well known in Chinese families that he must be respected. His Chinese name is Tai Tsui and it is absolutely vital you find out where he is residing each year. Once you know where he is located, make certain you do not incur his wrath by sitting in a direction that faces his direction. This means you are confronting him and you must never do that. You must never face him directly when you sit or work or eat. If you do, misfortune befalls you – even if that happens to be your best direction according to the Kua or Eight Mansions formula. Nor should you disturb his place with excessive noise, banging, digging, and renovations. If you do, the consequences are that you could get sick, suffer losses, lose out on important deals and opportunities, and generally feel rather sickly. So each year make an effort to determine his location. Here's a tip: the Grand Duke always resides in the place that corresponds to the animal sign of that year, and he occupies only fifteen degrees of the compass.

THE GRAND DUKE JUPITER resides as follows:

2001   *in the south-southeast (place of the snake)*
2002   *in the south (place of the horse)*
2003   *in the south-southwest (place of the sheep)*
2004   *in the west-southwest (place of the monkey)*
2005   *in the west (place of the rooster)*
2006   *in the west-northwest (place of the dog) and so on ...*

The Grand Duke's location during each of the 12 animal years of the lunar calendar follow the exact compass location of the animal year, so that in 2001, for instance, the Grand Duke resided in the compass location of the earthly branch of the animal sign of the snake, which means the 15 degrees defined as south-southeast. The direction of the Grand Duke is shown in the section on the 24 mountains in Part Two of this book. Note that his location moves in a clockwise direction around the compass and his direction is based on the earth plate where north is taken to mean magnetic north. Look at the illustration below ...

Usually, in any given year, the animal sign that is directly opposite the Grand Duke's location is said to be clashing with him. In the year of the horse, for instance, the animal sign of the rat clashes with the Tai Tsui, so those born in the year of the rat should appease the Grand Duke.

Traditionalists usually advise that one places the image or statue of the Pi Yao (also known as the Pi Kan or Pi Xie) inside the home in the direction of the Tai Tsui. This is believed to be a very effective cure to ensure that the Tai Tsui is not offended.

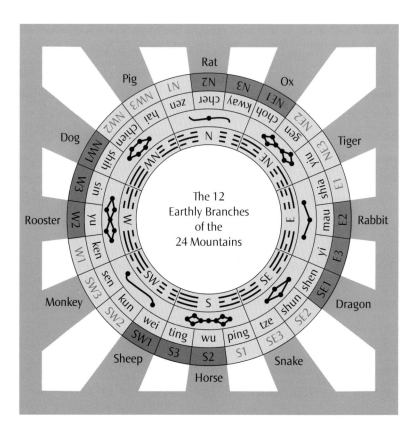

From the illustration opposite you can see that in 2003, the year of the sheep, those born in the year of the ox are affected.

My advice is to place a Pi Yao image (shown above) in the home since this is an auspicious celestial creature anyway – this way one never has to worry about offending the Grand Duke. The Pi Yao creature is available in a number of different postures.

30. EXHAUSTING THE NASTY FIVE YELLOW

The Five Yellow is also known as Wu Wang in Chinese and it is considered a very harmful affliction that can cause extreme damage to a family or company directly hit by it. It is something everyone doing business should be aware of. The Five Yellow is the number five of the annual flying star chart. It is easy to locate him if you can compile the charts. The Five Yellow occupies 45 degrees of the compass.

In 2001 – when the Lo Shu reigning number was 8 – the annual chart had 8 in the center and 5 in the southwest (see chart on the following page). So the Wu Wang was located in the southwest in the year 2001. Now note that the southwest belongs to the earth element as does the number 5, so in 2001 those hit by the Wu Wang really got it bad. This is because the southwest sector is adding strength to the affliction. Those who had their main door or their bedroom located in this sector would definitely suffer from the ill winds of the Wu Wang – unless they moved out of their afflicted bedroom or used another door to enter the house and closed the afflicted door altogether. If it is not possible to do either of these things then the only cure is to use metal windchimes. In 2001 six-rod windchimes were necessary (six is the number of metal, so enhancing its strength) because the Wu Wang was so strong. Otherwise a five-rod windchime would have sufficed. The use of metal exhausts earth. It does not destroy earth (wood destroys earth in the cycle of the elements). Note that in feng shui we always prefer to exhaust rather than destroy whenever we use the elements as cures. So to overcome the Wu Wang we use metal rather than wood.

As the chart below indicates, in 2002, the year of the horse, the reigning number has changed to 7, so the center number is 7, and the Wu Wang has flown to the east. Note also that in this year the annual chart is exactly the same as the period of seven chart (also with 7 in the center) so there is a double 5 in the annual chart. So although the Wu Wang in the east is nowhere near as harmful as it was in the southwest, nevertheless the double whammy will have an effect. It is less harmful in the east because this is a wood sector and wood destroys earth so the sector keeps the Wu Wang under control. In 2002 the windchime is not recommended as a cure because the metal will harm the intrinsic element of the east sector. So in 2002 you should avoid sleeping or working here.

In 2003 the Wu Wang is in the southeast, where the wood element also continues to keep it under control.

In 2004 it flies to the center of the house, where it becomes ferocious once more. This is because the five in the center is in its natural home. Note that in the original Lo Shu, five is in the center. This brings it into the heavenly heart of the home. If the center of the home has a room, then the Five Yellow is said to be imprisoned and thus cannot do any harm. However, in

SE	S	SW
7	3	5
6	8	1
2	4	9
NE	N	NW

E ... W

2001

SE	S	SW
6	2	4
5	7	9
1	3	8
NE	N	NW

E ... W

2002

homes where the center of the house is open – for instance if it is a family room, dining room, or living room, or if it houses the bedroom – it causes big problems for whoever stays in that room. The way to overcome it is to hang six-rod metal windchimes. For feng shui purposes hollow windchimes have the power to transform bad chi into good chi so hollow rods are preferable to solid rods. Note that the center of the home is said to belong to the earth sector so the Wu Wang, being in the center, is very strong. If windchimes seem insufficient you can also use six metal coins tied with gold ribbon and hung above a door that opens into the central room.

In 2005 the Five Yellow flies to the northwest where it is under control.

In 2006 it flies to the west where it is also under control. This is because both the northwest and west are metal sectors. Metal exhausts earth and is able to keep the Wu Wang under control.

So to summarize, when the Wu Wang occupies the sector of the house where the main door is, it becomes dangerous, irrespective of which compass sector this is. This is mainly because each act of opening and closing the door, or any kind of activity in the place of the Wu Wang, will activate its bad vibrations thereby causing misfortune. So do remember that when disturbed or activated it brings calamities, accidents, illness, or loss – or all of these in a battalion of troubles.

Like the other two afflictions the Five Yellow changes location each year, and where he resides in that year you must avoid the following:

- *Digging the ground. Doing so will cause you to get ill instantly.*
- *Cutting down any trees. Doing so activates the affliction immediately and you will get sick, have an accident, or your business will suffer a sudden setback which could be fatal.*
- *Disturbing that part of the land or house in any way, either with excessive noise, bright lights, or activity. Do not keep dogs or pets there as this activates it.*
- *Renovating that part of the house. This involves banging and digging and it is not advisable. If you need to do renovations to parts of the house that involve the sector with the Five Yellow, then make certain you do not start or end the renovation in the place of the Five Yellow.*

When disturbed the Five Yellow brings loss of wealth, loss of employment, accidents, injuries and calamities, robbery – and sometimes it can even bring death. The Five Yellow can take the form of the year star or the month star and when they occur in the same location at the same time, anyone residing in that corner of the home will immediately get ill. Of the two, however, the year Five Yellow is potentially the most dangerous so my strategy has always been to prepare myself at the start of each year. I do this by weakening the Five Yellow in the location where he is each year. To overcome the energy of the Five Yellow the best remedy is the six-rod all-metal windchime. Metal energy, and especially Yang metal which moves and makes sounds, will seriously weaken and exhaust the Five Yellow thereby reducing its harmful effects.

31. CONFRONTING THE THREE KILLINGS

The Three Killings direction is also known as the Saam Saat. You must never have this direction behind you at any time. So you must find out where it is each year and confront it boldly, otherwise it sends three types of misfortunes to disturb you and make your life miserable. It is part of feng shui practice to take note of where the Three Killings is located every year.

In 2003, the year of the sheep, the Three Killings is in the west. This means that during 2003 sitting with the direction west behind is foolish and deadly. This means you should not sit facing east. This holds even when the east is your best direction. You may, however, face the Three Killings directly. This means that in 2003 you can and should sit facing west. Confronting the Three Killings will not hurt you but having it behind you will. It is always more advantageous to sit facing the Three Killings head on.

When you are planning to do house repairs and renovations you must not do it in sectors that house the Three Killings. Thus in 2003 this means you should not undertake any renovations in the west part of your house You may, however, undertake renovations in sectors that are opposite the Three Killings.

The Three killings direction always occupies one of the four cardinal sectors – north, south, east, or west. So this is an affliction that covers 90 degrees of the compass. Here is a summary of where it flies to each year. Take note of these afflicted directions in each respective year and follow the advice never to have your back to this direction and never disturb it with renovations. If you have somehow inadvertently disturbed the Three Killings note the remedies given against the location information below.

Place of the Three Killings and how to fight it:

In Ox, Snake, and Rooster years the Three Killings is in the EAST (2201, 2005, 2009)
Antidote: Place a curved knife in the east during these years

In Pig, Rabbit, and Sheep years the Three Killings is in the WEST (2003, 2007, 2011)
Antidote: Place more bright lights in the west in these years

In Monkey, Rat, and Dragon years the Three Killings is in the SOUTH (2004, 2008, 2012)
Antidote: Place a large container of Yin (i.e. still) water in the south to overcome

In Dog, Horse, and Tiger years the Three Killings is in the NORTH (2002, 2006, 2010)
Antidote: Place three large boulders in the north during these years

風水

Flying Star Feng Shui

32. WHAT IS FLYING STAR FENG SHUI?

FLYING STAR FENG SHUI MAKES THE PRACTICE OF FENG SHUI COMPLETE. THE ANCIENT TEXTS ALWAYS REFER TO THE RELEVANCE OF PERIOD CYCLES OF TIME IN FENG SHUI. WE LOOKED CLOSELY AT TIME AFFLICTIONS OF PERIOD FENG SHUI IN THE PREVIOUS SECTION. IN THIS SECTION WE LOOK IN DEPTH AT FLYING STAR FENG SHUI AND HOW IT APPLIES TO HOMES AND BUILDINGS.

This approach to feng shui focuses on the significance of changing chi distribution in different time periods. The process highlights the intangible influences of environmental chi. These influences are expressed as numbers and combinations of numbers, which are cast into a natal chart. Interpreting the numbers in the different sectors is the basis of the practice of Flying Star feng shui.

The basic premise of flying star is that good luck or bad luck, i.e. harmony or disharmony in the environment, does not necessarily occur continuously or last forever. Nor do auspicious and inauspicious orientations remain throughout one's entire lifetime. Feng shui masters point to the rise and fall of dynasties to give credence to their conviction that there is a time element in feng shui practice that simply cannot be ignored.

Flying Star feng shui involves studying the influence of the earth's intangible forces in order to monitor annual and periodic changes in the feng shui luck of a house. This is Time Dimension feng shui. It alerts the practitioner to non-physical, invisible, and inauspicious time energy. Unless dealt with or countered this energy can cause serious misfortune to befall residents. Equally, there are auspicious forces and these must be activated for their full benefit to be felt.

Flying Star feng shui as a method of computation at first seems complex but in reality is quite easy. It is the interpretation of the numbers and their meanings that is not so easy to grasp or practice. There are also several special "rules" and "situations" which indicate the potential for immense luck, but unless activated these benefits do not materialize. So learning Flying Star feng shui places the potential for tremendous good fortune in the palm of your hand!

I have tried to ensure that what is contained in this book is as simplified as possible. I have included the Lo Shu natal charts of all houses built in this current period of seven as well as natal charts for the next period of eight. These are the most vital charts to become familiar with. In addition I have also introduced the concept of trigram houses, which is an easier branch of Flying Star feng shui. Trigram feng shui and annual charts are read together as combined charts. These will make it easier for amateur practitioners to graduate to the more complex flying star charts.

You will see that time dimension theory revolves around numbers and reflects the basic fundamentals of Chinese numerology. The main tool in the formulation and understanding of this theory is the original Lo Shu square, a symbol you are now familiar with. You have seen that the numbers in the Lo Shu move in a pre-arranged sequence which sets what I call the "flight path" for the way all other numbers "fly." These numbers have meanings. They signify the elements. They interact with each other and they interact significantly with the objects in the compass location where they are found.

These interactions are dynamic and they create intangible unseen forces that transform energy either into bad killing energy or into good, lucky energy. How to diagnose the relevant combination of numbers in various locations of the home is what Flying Star feng shui is about. To understand it thus requires one to understand the meanings of these numbers in a feng shui context, and then to interpret whether the numbers in each compass location bring good fortune or not – and, if not, what to do to counter their bad effect.

Both the methods introduced in this section require interpretation of numbers and combinations of numbers in the different compass sectors. Start by learning the number combinations in trigram feng shui before going on to the flying star natal charts.

33. TRIGRAM FENG SHUI AND ANNUAL CHARTS

In the last chapter we looked at time period annual and monthly charts in detail. We also closely examined the nine Lo Shu grids, each derived from the original Lo Shu square, and with a different reigning number in the center. Now we begin serious work in flying star natal chart feng shui.

There are different ways of creating the flying star natal chart of homes and buildings. In this book I am focusing on the two most popular methods. The first method is a simple technique where the chart is derived from the sitting direction of the home. The second method is the more comprehensive and widely used method where the natal chart is obtained from two sets of information – the facing orientation of the building and the time period the building is said to belong to. These two methods are integral components of time period feng shui and as you gain familiarity with both methods you will realize there is a great deal of similarity in the interpretations of the numbers.

The first method can loosely be called the trigram method. Here the chart of the house is based on its sitting direction. Here is how the trigram chart is created.

If you look again at the original Lo Shu square shown below, you will see that each direction has a corresponding number. In the trigram chart we first take note of the sitting direction of a house, then we see the number that corresponds to that direction. So you can see for instance that south is the number 9, north is the number 1, and so forth. Look at the numbers that correspond to all the other directions. To draw up the basic chart for any house we use a compass to check its sitting direction. Note that this is the exact opposite of

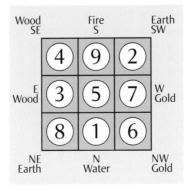

its facing direction. So if the facing direction is northwest it is sitting directly opposite i.e. southeast.

Another way of looking at this method is to say that it is based on the sitting trigram of the house. This is because the eight directions of the compass also correspond to one of the eight trigrams. You can check this out by looking at the Later Heaven Pa Kua illustrated in Part One of this book. As you go deeper into the various formulas you will appreciate the significance of the Pa Kua symbol, and its different attributes. Everything in the Pa Kua and the compass rings is interrelated.

So in this trigram method, houses are categorized into eight types for purposes of analysis, with each house being named for its sitting trigram and having a Lo Shu chart where the center number corresponds to its sitting trigram number. The eight different houses under this method will be illustrated later but first here is an example.

Here is a Li house which sits south and faces north. In this chart you can see instantly that the entrance sector where the house entrance is placed has the number 5, which is considered a troublesome and unlucky number. So in such a house it would appear to be advisable to move the entrance into the northwest sector so that it benefits from the benevolent number 1, which is a lucky number. In this house we also see the auspicious number 8 is located in the southeast and the auspicious 6 in the southwest. Later you can study the table on page 100, which gives a complete analysis of the numbers. For now look only at the single digit numbers of this chart. Note that the numbers by themselves do not mean much – they merely indicate

Lo Shu of a Li House

SE	S	SW
8	4	6
7	9	2
3	5	1
NE	N	NW

(E is at left of the middle row; W is at right of the middle row.)

the potential for good or bad luck to materialize. The luck (good as well as bad) will materialize when it is activated by annual and month stars or when there is the placement of symbolic objects that trigger the good or bad luck. Usually the placement of something protective will guard against bad luck and the placement of Yang energy – like the color red, happy lively music, and activity – can jump-start the good luck.

In terms of feng shui analysis, trigram charts are an excellent method of quickly examining the luck of houses by looking at how annual numbers, as well as monthly numbers, interact with the numbers of the trigram chart in each part of the house. Note that the grids of the Lo Shu square here and elsewhere in the book always refer to their compass location. Therefore the next step in the analysis is to place the annual number next to the chart numbers. Below is the chart of a Ken house which faces southwest and sits northeast. The larger numbers in the center represent the chart numbers of the sectors of the house. I have added the annual chart of the year 2003, the year of the sheep. These are the smaller numbers on the top right of the main number with 6 in the center. So then you can see how these numbers combine with the main chart numbers in every sector. Next I include a smaller number at the bottom right, to represent the second month of 2003.

How did I do this? I noted from the tables in the previous section that the Lo Shu reigning number for 2003 is 6 and the reigning number of the second month in that year is 4 (see page 81). With these two center numbers in place I am able to create a map of the luck of the various sectors of the house between March 6th and April 5th 2003.

Lo Shu of a Ken House

	SE	S	SW	
	7^{5}_{3}	3^{1}_{8}	5^{3}_{1}	
E	6^{4}_{2}	8^{6}_{4}	1^{8}_{6}	W
	2^{9}_{7}	4^{2}_{9}	9^{7}_{5}	
	NE	N	NW	

the luck of a Ken house in the 2nd month of 2003

I did this by systematically filling in all the numbers from grid to grid starting from the northwest, then to the west, and so on. One glance at this chart tells me that luck for this house in this month is moderate since the entrance sector (the southwest) has the auspicious number 1 star but the year star of number 3 will cause misunderstandings. However, the west sector is auspicious with the very lucky 1, 6, 8 combination.

34. INTERPRETING TRIGRAM CHARTS FROM YEAR TO YEAR

To use the trigram method, you have to determine what trigram house yours is. This requires the use of a compass to take directions. Take these readings at the main door, standing inside and facing squarely out. This direction is known as the facing direction of the house. It is indicated by the black arrow in the illustration below.

When you know the facing direction of your house you can determine its sitting direction. This is the direction opposite the facing direction. So when the house faces north it is sitting south and it will be a Li house. When a house faces east it is sitting west and is a Tui house and so forth. Each trigram house has its own reigning Lo Shu number, and from this number the chart of the house is generated based on the flight sequence of the numbers in the original Lo Shu square.

The table above identifies which of the eight trigrams applies to which type of house. Remember that the trigram is based on the sitting direction and this is the exact opposite of the facing direction. Identify the trigram that applies to your house.

The luck of the different sectors of the house is revealed in the combination of numbers of the house chart with those of the annual chart. To fine-tune, we can also include the numbers of the month charts. Opposite are some examples of trigram charts. They show the base chart of

TRIGRAM HOUSE	FACING DIRECTION	SITTING DIRECTION
A Li house	Is facing north	Is sitting south
A Kan house	Is facing south	Is sitting north
A Chen house	Is facing west	Is sitting east
A Tui house	Is facing east	Is sitting west
A Kun house	Is facing northeast	Is sitting southwest
A Chien house	Is facing southeast	Is sitting northwest
A Ken house	Is facing southwest	Is sitting northeast
A Sun house	Is facing northwest	Is sitting southeast

Lo Shu of a Li House

	SE	S	SW	
	8	4	6	
E	7	9	2	W
	3	5	1	
	NE	N	NW	

Lo Shu of a Chien House

	SE	S	SW	
	5	1	3	
E	4	6	8	W
	9	2	7	
	NE	N	NW	

Lo Shu of a Tui House

	SE	S	SW	
	6	2	4	
E	5	7	9	W
	1	3	8	
	NE	N	NW	

Lo Shu of a Sun House

	SE	S	SW	
	3	8	1	
E	2	4	6	W
	7	9	5	
	NE	N	NW	

the house only. To undertake the analysis of the luck of the house it is necessary to fill in the annual and month numbers into each grid as well. Only then can the charts reveal the luck of each sector for the year or month being investigated.

The luck of each of the nine sectors is then read in accordance with the meanings associated with the combination of the numbers. For easy reference the following table sets out the meanings of the combination of the house trigram and annual numbers. This is a very valuable table and learning the meanings of these numbers will go a long way towards bringing you success in your feng shui practice. You must understand that these meanings pertain to combinations of house chart numbers with annual star numbers. The meanings of some combinations here may appear similar to the meanings you will see later in flying star charts but they are not to be used interchangeably for the combinations of mountain and water stars that come later.

The Meanings of Trigram and Annual Number Combinations

THE TRIGRAM NUMBER	THE ANNUAL NUMBER	INDICATED DIVINATIONS AND OUTCOMES OF THE COMBINATION	ENHANCERS FOR GOOD LUCK COMBINATIONS OR REMEDIES FOR BAD LUCK COMBINATIONS
1	1	Excellent for academic study, research, and creative work. Good money luck. If afflicted by month star 5 or 2, there could be kidney-related illness. Accidents caused by excessive drinking and alcoholic problems	To enhance and also to control affliction, use six-rod windchimes
1	2	There could be marriage problems and a danger of loss of child through miscarriage. Beware of car accidents	Use plants to exhaust the water number 1 and strengthen earth element
1	3	Heartache caused by gossip and slandering. There could be lawsuits and legal entanglements	Use water to enhance and water plants
1	4	Political luck. Media and publicity luck. Romance luck, especially for women. Good writing luck for authors	Use slow-moving water but not too much
1	5	Health problems – sicknesses, food poisoning. Injury caused by accidents	Use a windchime
1	6	Excellent career luck. Promotion. Good money luck. Headaches, especially when month 5 or 2 comes in	Enhance with metal
1	7	Good money luck in period of 7. But it is also an indication that there will be cut-throat competition	Enhance with crystals or gem tree
1	8	Excellent wealth luck. There could be misunderstandings between loved ones, siblings, and good friends. Business partners have problems	Enhance with crystals

THE TRIGRAM NUMBER	THE ANNUAL NUMBER	INDICATED DIVINATIONS AND OUTCOMES OF THE COMBINATION	ENHANCERS FOR GOOD LUCK COMBINATIONS OR REMEDIES FOR BAD LUCK COMBINATIONS
1	9	Good for both career and money luck, but can turn bad when 5 flies in. Eye problems	Do not enhance
2	1	Stress develops in the marriage. Danger of miscarriage, accidents, and loss of a loved one	Use windchimes to control the bad star 2
2	2	Not a good indication. Magnifies strong negative feelings. Illness and accidents possible	Six-rod windchimes
2	3	Arguments and misunderstandings of the most severe kind. Back stabbing, hatred, legal disputes	Use still water to cool tempers. Do not disturb
2	4	Wives and mothers-in-law quarrel and fight. Disharmony. Good indications for writers and those in the journalism field. Good for those at school	Use water
2	5	Extremely inauspicious. Total loss and catastrophe. This is one of the most dangerous combinations in Flying star technology and, when the 5 flies in, anyone staying here can suddenly develop terminal illness	Use strong windchime (plenty). Beware, do not have fire or could result in death
2	6	Very easy life of ease and leisure, power and authority. This auspicious combination is spoilt if a five-rod windchime is placed here. The trinity (tien ti ren) gets activated in a negative way	Do not use windchimes. If there is sickness related to stomach place red amulet here

THE TRIGRAM NUMBER	THE ANNUAL NUMBER	INDICATED DIVINATIONS AND OUTCOMES OF THE COMBINATION	ENHANCERS FOR GOOD LUCK COMBINATIONS OR REMEDIES FOR BAD LUCK COMBINATIONS
2	7	There is money during the period of 7 but luck of children will not be good. Problems conceiving children. Unscrupulous people at work politic against you	Use metal (bells) and metal windchimes. Also hang sword of coins
2	8	Richness and wealth but there is ill health, although this is minor and can be remedied	Use water to overcome bad health star
2	9	Extremely bad luck. Nothing succeeds unless remedied. Not a good indication for children	Use water plants. Also use coins or windchime
3	1	Heartache due to gossip and slander. There could be lawsuits and legal entanglements	Use water to enhance and water plants
3	2	Dangerous for those in politics – lawsuits, even jail. Gossip, slander Bad luck for women, obesity	Some masters recommend gold and fire
3	3	Gossip and slander. Quarrels. Robbery possible	Use sword of coins
3	4	Heartache caused by sexual scandal	Use bright lights
3	5	Loss of wealth. Severe cash flow problems. If bedroom here, financial loss is severe. If kitchen is here sickness is inevitable. Do not stay here	Exhaust the 5 with copper mountain painting
3	6	Time of slow growth. Leg injuries. Bad for young males	Use Yin (still) water
3	7	You will get robbed or burgled. Violence. Possibility of injury from knives or guns. Blood	Use water

THE TRIGRAM NUMBER	THE ANNUAL NUMBER	INDICATED DIVINATIONS AND OUTCOMES OF THE COMBINATION	ENHANCERS FOR GOOD LUCK COMBINATIONS OR REMEDIES FOR BAD LUCK COMBINATIONS
3	8	Not good for children under 12 years. Danger to limbs	Use bright lights to cure
3	9	Robbery encounter. Lawsuits. Fights.	Use Yin (still) water
4	1	Very good romance luck but too much water leads to sex scandals. Affairs lead to unhappiness and breakup of family. Excellent creative and writing luck	Kuan Yin statue or image of laughing Buddha for some divine help
4	2	Illness of internal organs. Husband has affairs	Use amethysts
4	3	Emotional stress due to relationship and sex problems	Use red to overcome
4	4	Excellent for writing and creative luck. Very attractive to opposite sex. Romance will flourish	Fresh flowers to enhance growth of romance
4	5	Sexually transmitted skin diseases. Breast cancer	Use painting of water and mountain as cure
4	6	Money luck but creativity dries up. Bad luck indicated for women, especially pregnant women	Strengthen earth element with crystals
4	7	Bad luck in love. Will get cheated by opposite sex. Sickness of the thighs and lower abdomen	Use water to control
4	8	Excellent career luck for writers. Bad for very young children. Injury to limbs indicated	Use lights to combat

THE TRIGRAM NUMBER	THE ANNUAL NUMBER	INDICATED DIVINATIONS AND OUTCOMES OF THE COMBINATION	ENHANCERS FOR GOOD LUCK COMBINATIONS OR REMEDIES FOR BAD LUCK COMBINATIONS
4	9	A time for preparation. Good for students. Need to be careful of fire breaking out	Use wood or plants
5	1	Hearing problems and also sex-related illness	Use windchime
5	2	Misfortunes and extreme bad luck. Illness may be fatal	Use windchime
5	3	Money troubles. Disputes. Bad business luck	Use coins
5	4	Creativity dries up. Sickness. Skin problems	Use water/mountain
5	5	A very critical combination. Extreme danger indicated. Serious illness and accidents that can be fatal. Take care	Use metal six-rod windchimes to overcome
5	6	Bad financial luck. Loss. Diseases related to the head region. Danger also to the man	Place six coins under the carpet
5	7	Arguments abound. Mouth-related illness	Coins and bells
5	8	Problems related to the limbs, joints, and bones of the body. Be wary of rough sports	Use water to pacify
5	9	Bad luck all round. Do not speculate or gamble as you are sure to lose. Eye problems. Danger of fire	Use water
6	1	Financial luck and high achievers in the family. Headaches through excessive stress	Enhance with metal

THE TRIGRAM NUMBER	THE ANNUAL NUMBER	INDICATED DIVINATIONS AND OUTCOMES OF THE COMBINATION	ENHANCERS FOR GOOD LUCK COMBINATIONS OR REMEDIES FOR BAD LUCK COMBINATIONS
6	2	Great affluence and everything successful. Stomach problems. Patriarch could have sickness	No need to enhance but control with bells
6	3	Unexpected windfall. Speculative luck. Possible leg injury	Enhance with gemstones
6	4	Unexpected windfall for women of the family. Lower body injury. Pregnant women be careful	Enhance with crystals
6	5	Money luck blocked. Sickness could prevail	Use bells
6	6	Excellent money luck from heaven but too much metal can be dangerous, so do not enhance with metal	No need to enhance
6	7	Competitive squabbling over money. Arguments	Use water to curb
6	8	Wealth, popularity, prosperity. Great richness. Probably the best combination in Flying Star technique. Those in love are in for a lonely period	Enhance with water and make sure you have an entrance or window in that sector
6	9	Money luck. Frustration between generations – leading to arguments between young and old	Use water to reduce the frictions
7	1	Extremely good prosperity luck. Competition is deadly	Use water feature
7	2	Money luck dissipates. Children luck is dimmed	Use windchimes
7	3	Grave danger of injury to limbs. Be careful	Use water

THE TRIGRAM NUMBER	THE ANNUAL NUMBER	INDICATED DIVINATIONS AND OUTCOMES OF THE COMBINATION	ENHANCERS FOR GOOD LUCK COMBINATIONS OR REMEDIES FOR BAD LUCK COMBINATIONS
7	4	Taken for a ride by someone of the opposite sex. Pregnant women should take care	Use water
7	5	Problems due to excessive gossiping. Danger of poisoning or anything to do with the mouth	Use metal coins, bells, or windchimes
7	6	Negative chi – "sword fighting killing breath"	Use water
7	7	Victory over the competition. Money luck. Sex life gets a boost for young people. Beware of over-indulgence	Use water to curb excesses
7	8	Same as above but better	Use water
7	9	All troubles are caused through vulnerability to sexual advances. There is danger of fire hazards	Use earth (big boulders) to press down bad luck
8	1	Excellent and auspicious prosperity luck. Career advancement. Money luck, but sibling rivalry prevails	Enhance with water
8	2	Wealth creation possible. Properties and asset accumulation but danger of illness	Use mountain principle. Boulder tied with red thread
8	3	Move children away from this sector. Limb injuries	Use red, yellow
8	4	Overpowering matriarch. Love life of younger generation suffer from mother problems. Limb injuries	Use fire or red to overcome
8	5	Problems related to the limbs, joints, and bones of the body. Be careful of rough sports	Use water to pacify

THE TRIGRAM NUMBER	THE ANNUAL NUMBER	INDICATED DIVINATIONS AND OUTCOMES OF THE COMBINATION	ENHANCERS FOR GOOD LUCK COMBINATIONS OR REMEDIES FOR BAD LUCK COMBINATIONS
8	6	Wealth, popularity, prosperity. Great richness. One of the best combinations in Flying Star system. Love life goes through a rough patch	Enhance with crystals, make sure there's an entrance or window in that sector
8	7	Prevail over the competition. Money luck. Sex life gets a boost for young people. Beware over-indulgence	Use water to curb excesses
8	8	Excellent wealth creation luck. Very favorable	No need to enhance
8	9	Excellent for money and celebration but misunderstandings between the young and older generation can turn nasty	Use water to calm the fire
9	1	Good for both career and money luck, but can turn bad when 5 flies in. Eye problems	Do not enhance
9	2	Extremely bad luck. Nothing succeeds unless remedied. Not a good indication for children	Use water plants. Also use coins or windchime
9	3	Robbery encounter. Lawsuits. Fights. Fire hazard	Use Yin (still) water
9	4	A time for preparation. Good for students. Careful of fire	Use wood or plants
9	5	Bad luck all round. Do not speculate or gamble as you are sure to lose. Eye problems. Danger of fire	Use water
9	6	Money luck. Frustration between generations leading to arguments between young and old	Water to reduce the frictions

THE TRIGRAM NUMBER	THE ANNUAL NUMBER	INDICATED DIVINATIONS AND OUTCOMES OF THE COMBINATION	ENHANCERS FOR GOOD LUCK COMBINATIONS OR REMEDIES FOR BAD LUCK COMBINATIONS
9	7	Troubles caused through vulnerability to sexual advances. There is danger of fire	Use earth (big boulders) to press down bad luck
9	8	Excellent for money and celebration. But misunderstandings between the young and older generation can turn nasty	Use water to calm the fire
9	9	Good or bad depending on other indications	Do not enhance

In the next section, when you learn how to cast the natal chart of the house under the more comprehensive Flying Star method, you will be introduced to the powerful concept of water and mountain star numbers which will take your practice of feng shui a step higher. I do not need to tell you the great value of knowing these feng shui formulas. It is like having a secret edge over others. Your ability to fine-tune your luck puts you in control of your life. You can plan the timing of all your important activities and, as those who know anything about management, investment, or even speculative activity will be aware, nothing gives you a better competitive edge than to be able to fine-tune your timing. In most instances perfect timing is the key to success!

With flying star, your reading of the feng shui of any house will be as near to being complete as anyone can make it. Hopefully by then you will also know how to analyze your surrounding environment, how to protect your home from bad chi, and how to activate good chi. Then you will not need an outsider to do your feng shui for you – you will be able to do it yourself.

Remember, no one has perfect feng shui – certainly not all the time. The passage of months and years influences the ups and downs in our lives. It is the same with feng shui. The clever attitude is to work at enhancing the highs so we may all live to our fullest potential, and making the lows tolerable so we don't get floored when things look bad for us.

35. CONSTRUCTING FLYING STAR NATAL CHARTS

Before we start to construct a flying star natal chart let me introduce you to a typical flying star chart. Note that the "stars" referred to are actually numbers, with each number representing and signifying various attributes. In each of the nine sectors there is a main star number, a mountain star number, and a water star number (we'll look at these in detail later). These star numbers are different in each sector of the grid. Look at the typical Lo Shu flying star natal chart illustrated below. It shows a period of seven house (so the main numeral 7 is in the center) with its main door located in the south sector and the door facing the first mountain of the south direction i.e. S1 mountain.

The water star is the small number on the right of each sector of the grid. Note here that the water star in the center grid is 2 and this tells me the house is facing south (the main number of the south grid is 2). The mountain star is the small number on the left of each sector. Note that the mountain star in the center is 3. This tells me the house is sitting north (because the main number in the north is 3). The plus or minus sign next to the center water and mountain stars depends on whether the center numbers are odd or even, and also which sub-directions, 1, 2, or 3 the house facing direction is. In this case the sub-direction of this house is obviously S1, because the odd mountain star 3 flies plus and the even water star number 2 flies minus.

Flying Star feng shui examines all the numbers in all the nine sectors and draws conclusions about the luck of the sectors of a dwelling place during a specific time period. All this analysis is based on the numbers that come together in each sector. These nine sectors of the grid are known as the nine palaces.

	SE	S	SW	
	2 3 **6**	7 7 **2**	9 5 **4**	
E	1 4 **5**	3⁺ 2⁻ **7**	5 9 **9**	**W**
	6 8 **1**	8 6 **3**	4 1 **8**	
	NE	N	NW	

The scope of the flying star technique is quite awesome. This is an advanced method of investigating the luck of any house at any time. Once you have the natal chart of any house or building, you can analyze how the luck of the residents will ebb and flow very accurately.

The forecasting dimension comes in because you can actually analyze the chart to see what the luck of the house will be in every month or every year, and take measures accordingly. This is the method most authentic feng shui masters use. How good a feng shui master is depends on how good he or she is in analyzing the numbers and in activating the good numbers, while diffusing the bad numbers.

You can use the natal chart to investigate the luck of any corner of any room in the house. To take it further, experts can also use flying star to analyze the luck of different parts of a city or of a country when they are skilled enough to work out the natal chart of the area. This is not easy to do and is not within the scope this book.

Computing the flying star natal chart

Computation must be done correctly. If the computation of the star numerals is incorrect, the analyses will be flawed to the extent that serious mistakes can result. To ensure accuracy of practice the explanation of the steps is illustrated with examples.

Step One: Determine the period

Begin by determining the period in which your house was built or when it was last renovated. Thus if your house was built in 1946 that makes it a period five house (see part one on time periods) and the starting point is a Lo Shu square with the number 5 in the center. However, if the house was extensively renovated say in 1975, this renovation will transform it into a period six house and hence the number 6 will appear in the center. Determining the period of the house gives you the base chart with all the main base numbers set out in the nine palaces.

Now exactly what constitutes a renovation, or how a house changes period, is a fairly controversial issue among feng shui masters. It seems that there are differences of opinion that present serious consequences on the chart used for analysis. Because this is quite a controversial issue we will look at it in detail a little later.

So the first step is selecting the Lo Shu grid that applies to your house. If your house was built in 1990 or renovated in 1990, for example, then you are living in a period of seven house and the Lo Shu base chart to use is the one with the number 7 in the center.

The Lo Shu with 5 in the center is the original Lo Shu. If your house was built between 1944 and 1963, or if this was the time when it was last renovated, then to cast your natal chart you should use a Lo Shu square with 5 in the center as this was the period of five. If, however, your house was renovated after 1963 you will have to move on to the Lo Shu square which reflects the new period of the house. Note that old houses of a previous period have what is known as very "tired energy." The chi is weak and luck is usually limited. When you renovate your house you are revitalizing it.

Note the period of six base chart below. Note the number 6 in the center of the square. Because the number in the center has changed, all the other numbers also change. It is useful for you to see how the numbers change because this charts the flight of the numbers i.e. how 5 becomes 6, and 6 becomes 7, 7 becomes 8, and so forth. Once you familiarize yourself with the "flight" of the numbers, you will start to discern the pattern of the movement. So far we are seeing the numbers move in an ascending order and this is known as flying in a Yang mode. Numbers can also fly in a Yin mode when it comes to the mountain and water stars. This is denoted by the plus or minus sign against the water and mountain stars.

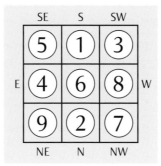

SE	S	SW
4	9	2
3 (E)	5	7 (W)
8	1	6
NE	N	NW

Period 5

SE	S	SW
5	1	3
4 (E)	6	8 (W)
9	2	7
NE	N	NW

Period 6

SE	S	SW
6	2	4
5 (E)	7	9 (W)
1	3	8
NE	N	NW

Period 7

In the period of seven base chart the number in the center has become 7 and again, as a result of this, all the numbers in the other sectors of the square have also changed. This is the Lo Shu to use for all houses or buildings built or renovated between 1984 and 2003. This makes this also the Lo Shu of this period. During the period of seven, 7 is an auspicious number. Later on when we come to the interpretation of natal charts you will see that the number that signifies the current period is considered an exceptionally lucky number. So 7 is lucky until 2003, but when we change to period eight in 2004, the number 7 turns unlucky.

When deciding on which Lo Shu square is the correct one to use for your house, you might be fazed by the term "renovation." Not all feng shui masters agree on what constitutes a renovation. Certain flying star experts have indicated to me that only a major renovation that involves the addition of new floor space or the changing of the entire roof with a lot of banging and building qualifies as a renovation in flying star analysis. This is the kind of renovation that is strong enough to change the flying star period and hence the center number of the Lo Shu square.

Other masters insist that a repainting and change in the soft furnishings of the house is sufficient to count as a renovation. I believe this is a matter of personal judgment. Personally, I do not consider a repaint and interior décor job a renovation but I do not think one has to change the roof to qualify for the term renovation. As long as there is banging, drilling, tearing down of walls, and rebuilding of some parts of the house this should count as renovation. Thus if you have done something like this to your house any time between 1984 and 2003 then, irrespective of when your house was built, yours will qualify as a period of seven house, and the main star numeral in the center will be 7. This will be your starting point.

A recent development in this issue has arisen since I last wrote about flying star. It seems that one of the most respected feng shui masters has now decided that one does not even need to renovate a house to change its period. All that is needed, according to this famous practitioner, is that the house be left empty for one hundred days! This interpretation, if correct, is good news for apartment dwellers who have little or no control over the period change of the whole building that houses their apartment. Now, according to the new interpretation, to change the period of their apartment (and this is becoming crucial with period eight just around the corner) all they need do is move out of their apartment for 100 days, and then move back in again. Leaving the apartment empty will cause its energy to wilt. Moving in again introduces new energy. (More on this later when we discuss changing to period eight).

Step Two: Determine the facing direction of the house

There is also some controversy surrounding the next step in the construction of the flying star chart. This involves determining the facing direction of the house. Usually the facing direction of the house is the same as the facing direction of its main door but this need not always be the case (see page 37 for the various criteria for determining the facing direction of your home). Once you have decided which is the direction that best describes the way your house faces, use a reliable compass to measure this direction.

You should take the direction three times on a compass you are familiar with. Stand just inside the house, or at the doorway of the house, then three feet inside and next perhaps three feet outside. You will have to find a convenient place to determine this facing direction accurately. The three directions taken could be different and this is quite normal. Small variances are to be expected since compass readings are affected by magnetic energy caused by the presence of metallic objects.

Most flying star masters now agree that it is the house facing direction that determines the flying star chart. Note that the facing direction:

a *need not be the same as the facing direction of the main door*
b *is usually the direction in front of which is empty space or busy Yang energy*
c *for apartments is the facing direction of the whole building*
d *can sometimes be the direction where there is a large balcony or picture window*

On-site investigation is vital in difficult cases. There are houses that come in irregular shapes, that are modular in concept, and which may have several different wings. In such instances experience does help, but I have to say that I have come across buildings which are simply impossible to analyze with flying star charts. For example in the case of houses or apartment buildings that have no clear-cut facing direction, or which have so many entrances that one gets confused instantly. In such cases my experience has been that the chi also gets confused, and luck is, at best, erratic.

When you take directions do be accurate. Take note of emptiness lines and yin gaps, then determine which of the eight directions and which of the 24 mountains of the earth plate best measures the house facing direction. For example if the house faces east, then take note of this but also note which of the three sub-directions of east it faces i.e. E1, E2, or E3. Both pieces of information are required to cast the natal chart because it is the main facing direction that determines the number of the water star in the center and the sub-direction it faces that determines whether the water star numbers move from sector to sector in an ascending or a descending order i.e. in a plus mode or a minus mode.

Step Three: Determine the center number of water and mountain stars

The next step is to determine the center number of the water star (the siang sin) and the mountain star (the chor sin). First obtain the center number of the water star – this is the number of the facing direction of the house. The center mountain star number is the number of the house sitting direction. This is always the number opposite the facing direction. So when the facing direction of the house is east, its sitting direction is west. When the facing direction is north the sitting direction is south. To obtain the numbers that represent the direction we look at the period chart of the house. So if it is a period seven house we look a period seven chart.

Examples: We'll now look at the flying star charts of two period seven houses, the first one facing east, and the second facing northwest. Let me guide you through how the water and mountain stars are placed in the center.

PERIOD SEVEN HOUSE FACING EAST in sub-section E1

1. *Note the number of the EAST grid is 5.*
2. *This becomes the center number of the water stars.*
3. *Since 5 is an odd number the flight path of the water stars around the whole chart flies plus, minus, minus. This means it flies plus when the house facing direction is E1, and it flies minus when the house facing direction is E2 or E3. In this case since the house is facing E1 the water stars fly plus i.e. in an ascending order.*
4. *So the water star in the northwest sector is 6, and in the west sector is 7 and so on. The gray arrows show the flight path of the water stars. It continues on to 8 in the northeast, 9 in the south, 1 in the north, 2 in the southwest, 3 in the east, and 4 in the southeast.*
5. *Next look at number opposite east 5. This is west and the number is 9. This is the sitting direction number and it becomes the mountain star number in the center.*

Period 7 House Facing E1

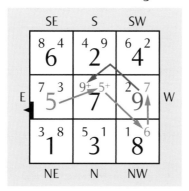

6. *Since the number of the mountain star is odd, its flight path is exactly the same as that of the water star. So the next mountain star from the center which is in the northwest is the number 1, ascending from 9. In the next sector, west, the mountain star is 2 and so on.*

See if you can work out the number of the mountain stars in the other palaces of the whole chart. Remember to move in the same sequence as the water stars moved. In this example the numbers are changing in an ascending manner from sector to sector because the numbers are moving in a Yang plus mode.

Placing all the water stars and mountain stars on the right and left of the main star numbers completes the flying star chart. By analyzing this chart a great deal of extremely useful information about the luck of this house can be revealed. In this book all the period seven flying star natal charts have been cast for easy reference. So if you are having a hard time learning how to cast the natal chart you can skip this section and move straight to the analysis section. For those determined to master the method let us move on to another example.

PERIOD SEVEN HOUSE FACING NORTHWEST in sub-section NW1

This period seven house faces northwest, where the main number is 8. The number 8 therefore becomes the center number of the water star. Because this number is even the water star numbers will fly minus, plus, plus. In this case since the door faces NW1, the water stars fly in a descending fashion, i.e. minus.

Period 7 House Facing NW1

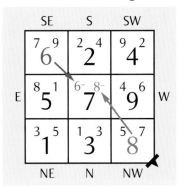

So water star 8 in the next palace from the center, which is northwest, becomes 7, and it becomes 6 in the west, 5 in the northeast and so on ...

The sitting direction is southeast, and here the main number is 6. This becomes the mountain star number in the center. Because 6 is an even number it flies minus, plus, plus. Since this house is facing the first sub-direction NW1, the stars will fly in a minus fashion i.e. descending. So the center mountain star of 6 becomes 5 in the northwest, 4 in the west, 3 in the northeast and so on ... Note that both water and mountain stars fly in the same sequential arrangement as the main star numbers.

To ensure you do not get confused please take note of the following pointers:

* *Note that when we look at period charts the numbers in the nine palaces are no longer in their original Lo Shu arrangement. The numbers in the nine palaces have "moved" – and so the three numbers in a row no longer add up to 15.*
* *The numbers from the center outwards do not move in a haphazard manner. Every one of the "stars" or numbers from 1 to 9 always change around the nine palaces in a set pattern. This follows the placement of numbers in the original Lo Shu square with the number 5 in the center. Every feng shui practitioner who wants to practice Flying Star feng shui must commit this flight pattern to memory. To practice, all you need to do is look at the way the numbers change from one palace to the next.*
* *Remember the flight of the water and mountain stars can be ascending or descending – what we term plus or minus. To determine if the numbers fly plus or minus just remember that odd*

numbers fly plus, minus, minus for 1st, 2nd, and 3rd sub-directions. Even numbers fly minus, plus, plus for the 1st, 2nd, and 3rd directions. This rule is true for period seven charts. But in the period of eight (and in some other period charts) there is an exception to this rule, and I will cover this when we reach the section on changing to period eight.

Summary of steps in casting a flying star natal chart

Differentiate between the period of the house or building to establish the base chart
Determine the facing direction of the house or building
Determine the sub-direction of the facing direction
Determine the center numbers of the water stars and mountain stars
Determine if these center numbers of the water and mountain stars are odd or even
Determine if the water and mountain stars are flying plus or minus
Fly the water stars i.e. fill in the water star numbers in the nine palaces
Fly the mountain stars i.e. fill in the mountain star numbers in the nine palaces
The next step is to superimpose the flying star natal chart onto the house layout plan for analysis.

36. WATER STARS AND MOUNTAIN STARS

Many expert practitioners of Flying Star feng shui focus only on the combination of the water star numbers and mountains star numbers in each of the nine palaces, and especially in the palaces where the main door and the master bedroom are located. And indeed these two stars reveal vital dimensions relating to the wealth, health, and happiness luck of the residents. Here are the basic attributes of these two stars, which are useful to bear in mind when we go deeper into flying star chart analysis in the next section.

The water star (also known as the siang sin star)

The water, or siang sin, star symbolizes wealth and prosperity prospects. It also signifies the career luck, financial status, growth, and business prospects of the residents. Since it is said to be symbolic of riches, having an auspicious water star in the sector where your front door, office, study, or master bedroom is, is said to bring you the luck of wealth and prosperity. Thus if the main door is located where the number 7 or number 8 siang sin star is found during the period of seven, it is a very auspicious sign for all the residents of the household in that period.

Such auspicious water stars are said to be hugely magnified under certain circumstances that serve to "activate" the water star. For instance, when the door faces an open area and there is an auspicious water star there the chi is extremely lucky. It improves further with the presence of water and such residents will definitely become extremely wealthy during the period of seven. Luck is further improved when some form of water, like a small fishpond or a fountain, is also placed in the corners of living and dining rooms that correspond to the auspicious water star sector. So knowing where the auspicious water star numbers are located in the house, as well as in each of the corners of all the rooms of the house, goes a long way to enhancing the wealth luck of the house. The key lies in correctly identifying the palace that has the luckiest water star.

The mountain star (also known as the chor sin star)

The chor sin star is said to govern the health prospects of the house, as well as relationship luck, romance, love, family authority, and mental attitudes. Its great significance is based on its number in the various palaces in the flying star natal chart of any house. The number that is assigned to each of the chor sin stars in the different palaces indicates the quality of the resident's health, social standing, and popularity during any period of time. Thus when the mountain star number in the palace that houses the main door or the bedroom is afflicted, then health takes a turn for the worse. Afflicted mountain stars are the numbers 5 or 2. These numbers indicate sickness and severe ill health that can be fatal during any month and year where the flying star number 5 or 2 also happen to fly into the same palace.

An auspicious chor sin star is one that corresponds to the number of the period under review. Thus in the period of seven, the chor sin star that is numbered 7 is auspicious. There are also other auspicious numbers associated with the mountain star, the most important of which is the number 8.

Flying star analysis, however, goes far beyond merely looking at the mountain and water stars in isolation. What is important is to see the way the numbers combine. Basically there are three sets of number combinations that are important when analyzing flying star charts. These are:

1 The water and mountain star combinations
2 The water star and the base star combinations
3 The mountain star and the base star combinations

In undertaking the above analysis, we must look at the following:

1   The meanings of the numbers

2   The meanings of the number combinations

3   The meanings of the element interactions of the star numbers

4   The meanings of the element interactions on the palaces

5   The strength of the numbers based on the period

6   Special advanced methods of analysis

It is vital to note that for residents to feel the full impact of all the star numbers, be they good or bad, they have to be activated. Water stars are activated by activity; by the presence of water, valleys, holes, or lower land; and by the presence of certain symbols. When the water star number is an unlucky number, activating it causes loss of wealth and when the star number is auspicious activating it brings wealth luck.

Mountain stars are activated by stillness and quiet, and by the presence of "mountains," crystals, statues, sculptures, and ceramic symbols of good fortune. Once again, when the mountain star numbers are unlucky, activating them with stones, boulders, or higher land causes severe illness to ripen, while activating auspicious mountain star numbers brings fame, recognition, victory, authority, power, or popularity.

37. PERIOD OF SEVEN CHARTS

To enable readers to get the most out of this book as both an instructional and a reference manual I have reproduced all 16 of the period of seven flying star natal charts (these can be found on page 120). Each facing direction has two charts that take account of the three sub-directions. Feng shui practitioners may use these charts to undertake detailed analysis of period seven houses and buildings. Those whose homes or buildings are of an earlier period can easily construct the flying star chart applicable to their period. Please note, however, that in the light of the new interpretations on renovations and changing the period of houses, it is safe to say that since we are now at the tail end of the period of seven, it is more than likely that most people will be staying in period of seven homes. What we need to reflect on then is what we should do to prepare for the coming change of period to period eight on 4 February 2004 (this is dealt with in Part Seven).

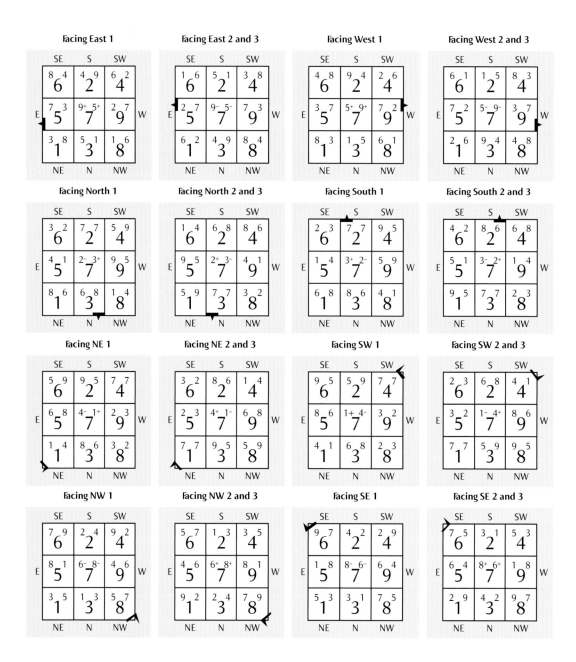

Facing East 1

SE	S	SW
8 4 — 6	4 9 — 2	6 2 — 4
7 3 — 5 (E)	9+ 5+ — 7	2 7 — 9 (W)
3 8 — 1	5 1 — 3	1 6 — 8
NE	N	NW

Facing East 2 and 3

SE	S	SW
1 6 — 6	5 1 — 2	3 8 — 4
2 7 — 5 (E)	9- 5- — 7	7 3 — 9 (W)
6 2 — 1	4 9 — 3	8 4 — 8
NE	N	NW

Facing West 1

SE	S	SW
4 8 — 6	9 4 — 2	2 6 — 4
3 7 — 5 (E)	5+ 9+ — 7	7 2 — 9 (W)
8 3 — 1	1 5 — 3	6 1 — 8
NE	N	NW

Facing West 2 and 3

SE	S	SW
6 1 — 6	1 5 — 2	8 3 — 4
7 2 — 5 (E)	5- 9- — 7	3 7 — 9 (W)
2 6 — 1	9 4 — 3	4 8 — 8
NE	N	NW

Facing North 1

SE	S	SW
3 2 — 6	7 7 — 2	5 9 — 4
4 1 — 5 (E)	2- 3+ — 7	9 5 — 9 (W)
8 6 — 1	6 8 — 3	1 4 — 8
NE	N	NW

Facing North 2 and 3

SE	S	SW
1 4 — 6	6 8 — 2	8 6 — 4
9 5 — 5 (E)	2+ 3- — 7	4 1 — 9 (W)
5 9 — 1	7 7 — 3	3 2 — 8
NE	N	NW

Facing South 1

SE	S	SW
2 3 — 6	7 7 — 2	9 5 — 4
1 4 — 5 (E)	3+ 2- — 7	5 9 — 9 (W)
6 8 — 1	8 6 — 3	4 1 — 8
NE	N	NW

Facing South 2 and 3

SE	S	SW
4 2 — 6	8 6 — 2	6 8 — 4
5 1 — 5 (E)	3- 2+ — 7	1 4 — 9 (W)
9 5 — 1	7 7 — 3	2 3 — 8
NE	N	NW

Facing NE 1

SE	S	SW
5 9 — 6	9 5 — 2	7 7 — 4
6 8 — 5 (E)	4- 1+ — 7	2 3 — 9 (W)
1 4 — 1	8 6 — 3	3 2 — 8
NE	N	NW

Facing NE 2 and 3

SE	S	SW
3 2 — 6	8 6 — 2	1 4 — 4
2 3 — 5 (E)	4+ 1- — 7	6 8 — 9 (W)
7 7 — 1	9 5 — 3	5 9 — 8
NE	N	NW

Facing SW 1

SE	S	SW
9 5 — 6	5 9 — 2	7 7 — 4
8 6 — 5 (E)	1+ 4- — 7	3 2 — 9 (W)
4 1 — 1	6 8 — 3	2 3 — 8
NE	N	NW

Facing SW 2 and 3

SE	S	SW
2 3 — 6	6 8 — 2	4 1 — 4
3 2 — 5 (E)	1- 4+ — 7	8 6 — 9 (W)
7 7 — 1	5 9 — 3	9 5 — 8
NE	N	NW

Facing NW 1

SE	S	SW
7 9 — 6	2 4 — 2	9 2 — 4
8 1 — 5 (E)	6- 8- — 7	4 6 — 9 (W)
3 5 — 1	1 3 — 3	5 7 — 8
NE	N	NW

Facing NW 2 and 3

SE	S	SW
5 7 — 6	1 3 — 2	3 5 — 4
4 6 — 5 (E)	6+ 8+ — 7	8 1 — 9 (W)
9 2 — 1	2 4 — 3	7 9 — 8
NE	N	NW

Facing SE 1

SE	S	SW
9 7 — 6	4 2 — 2	2 9 — 4
1 8 — 5 (E)	8- 6- — 7	6 4 — 9 (W)
5 3 — 1	3 1 — 3	7 5 — 8
NE	N	NW

Facing SE 2 and 3

SE	S	SW
7 5 — 6	3 1 — 2	5 3 — 4
6 4 — 5 (E)	8+ 6+ — 7	1 8 — 9 (W)
2 9 — 1	4 2 — 3	9 7 — 8
NE	N	NW

Interpreting Flying Star Charts

PART FIVE

38. MEANINGS OF THE NINE STAR NUMBERS

EACH OF THE NUMBERS ONE TO NINE HAS INTRINSIC ATTRIBUTES THAT GIVE AN INSIGHT INTO THE QUALITY OF ENERGY. THESE ATTRIBUTES CAN BE STRENGTHENED OR WEAKENED BY THE PASSAGE OF TIME, DEPENDING ON WHAT PERIOD WE ARE LIVING THROUGH. THESE NUMBERS CAN ALSO STAY DORMANT OR THEY CAN COME TO LIFE. AND FINALLY, THESE NUMBERS CAN SHOW A YIN OR A YANG ASPECT EVEN THOUGH THEY INTRINSICALLY POSSESS A YIN OR A YANG CHARACTER.

The numbers one to nine are described in terms of their colors. They are given names and they have places in the constellation of the Big Dipper. Most importantly, all these numbers have meanings. Each number has a negative and positive connotation, and an auspicious and inauspicious aspect. These aspects manifest when the numbers are activated.

While flying star numbers show benevolent faces, they really get activated with a vengeance when certain physical structures within the environment trigger off their attributes. When you understand the nature of each number and all the connotations and attributes associated with them you will realize that Chinese feng shui in effect incorporates the science of numbers as well.

The meanings attributed to the numbers one to nine have been extracted from old Chinese manuals and simplified for ease of application. You can use them to interpret the auspicious and inauspicious sectors of any home or building for the period of seven (1984–2003) or for any period in the coming years. Refer to the period seven house charts opposite to practice. Try to develop an easy familiarity with the numbers – after all there are only nine to memorize.

The auspicious numbers

The most auspicious numbers are said to be the reigning number of the relevant period and the numbers 1, 6, and 8.

The **number 1** represents long-gone prosperity but, because it represents water and water means wealth or money, it is regarded favorably. It is also a white number and all white numbers are auspicious. The number 1 signifies the start of a new beginning. It symbolizes things getting better after having been bad. The number 1 as a water star number is especially auspicious because 1 stands for the element of water. When it enters the east and the southeast the number 1 manifests its "greedy wolf" persona. This is the name of 1 in the Big Dipper or symbol of nine stars in the constellations. The number 1 has a positive as well as a negative side. When it shows its good side the number 1 indicates success at a young age, fame, and smart kids for the home. When the number 1 shows its bad side it can manifest as harm coming to the wife. This happens when it flies into the southwest as a mountain star. It can also cause blindness when it clashes with the fire energy of the south. This means it shows up as the mountain star in the south palace of the house. Sometimes such a configuration can also lead to premature death. The number 1 has a strong effect on the fortunes of the middle son and, when it flies into the north, it brings either enhanced income to the son or marriage opportunities.

The **number 6** represents faded prosperity but because it symbolizes the trigram Chien, which means gold, it also means riches and prosperity. In fact the number 6 is highly prized and every time it occurs in the northwest sector, the patriarch of the home benefits and is said to be going through a good period. It is generally regarded as the number that signifies heaven. It is also a white star, and in the constellation of the Big Dipper the number 6 represents finance and everything to do with money. At its most positive, 6 brings or represents high authority, influence, and great riches. When negative, the number 6 harms and exhausts the wife. In very bad instances where the 6 is severely afflicted it can cause death.

The **number 8**, during the period of seven, represents future prosperity because it is the reigning number of the next period. But 8 is also regarded as a very lucky number, which will continue to be lucky for the forthcoming 20 years. In fact the number 8, which is also a white star, is entering into its brightest period. This comes only once in 180 years so it is advisable to take full advantage of the coming period of 8. To activate the luck of this number, it should be

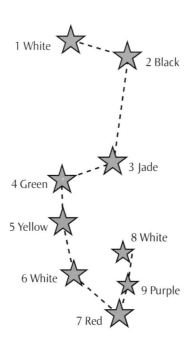

1 White
2 Black
3 Jade
4 Green
5 Yellow
8 White
6 White
9 Purple
7 Red

soaked in Yang energy. When there is movement, sound, and activity, the number 8 brings a great deal of good fortune. In the Big Dipper constellation 8 is known as the Left Assistant. It benefits most the youngest son of the family and, at its most positive, 8 signifies great wealth, honesty, and nobility. At its most negative, or when it gets afflicted either by harmful structures in the environment or by the presence of excessive metal energy, 8 can harm children and cause sickness to manifest.

The number 4 is the intelligence star. The number 4 signifies excellent writing skills and the attainment of exceptional academic excellence. In the constellation of nine stars this number also stands for literary pursuits. All these positive attributes occur throughout the nine periods but in varying strengths. It is strongest during the period of 4. In the present period seven and the coming period eight, the number 4 is not unlucky but its strength is not as potent. When 4 transforms into a dead star, it can cause residents residing in the palace to be driven to severe mental stress, unless it is combined with an unafflicted white star. The number 4 is a dead star during the lower periods of 7, 8, and 9, but when combined with 1, for instance, it comes alive and unleashes its positive benefits.

The **number 7** represents current prosperity and when 7 enters into the facing palace where the main door is located, it is said to bring exceptional good fortune during the period of seven. Because 7 is such an important number until the year 2003, it should be activated by placing a clock, a pendulum, or any other moving object in the palace of the house which has 7 either as the water, mountain, or base star during this period. If the two stars, the water and the mountain, have 7 in the sector of your main door, it is an extremely auspicious indication which can also be magnified and enhanced in several different ways, depending on which type of luck one wishes. If you want wealth then it is a good idea to activate the water star 7 by introducing the presence of water. In the Big Dipper constellation 7 is known as the Broken Soldier – and 7 manifests this aspect when we move into the period of eight. Then it transforms into a most vicious and dangerous number, indicating bloodshed and violence caused by metal chi. This is because 7 is a metal number and its color in the constellation is red. In terms of the member of the family, it signifies the youngest daughter. So when 7 is auspicious it promises riches and benefits the youngest child, especially the daughter of the family. When it turns nasty, however, 7 causes robbery, violence, and death. It can also signify loss of a family member, imprisonment, and even accidents caused by fire.

The number 9 represents distant prosperity. This is because 9 is the reigning number of the 20-year period of the distant future i.e. from the years 2024 to 2043. Nine is the purple star and in the constellation it is known as the Right-hand Assistant. Nine expands and multiplies all good or bad fortune equally. It is a big-hearted star. It nurtures and it helps the matriarch to care for the family. It is supportive of earth numbers like 2, 5, and 8. This means that when it is combined with 2 or 5 it expands their malevolence, but when combined with 8 it multiplies the good fortune. The number 9 can be regarded as lucky on its own. Much like 8, this number is a perennial favorite with the Chinese. The number 9 denotes the fire element and is especially auspicious when it occurs as a mountain star in any one of the earth sectors southwest or northeast. The number 9 is also a number that cannot change or be corrupted. Irrespective of how many times you multiply 9, the sum of its digits always add up to 9. So, at its most Yang and favorable, 9 brings fame and recognition, success and fruition. At its most negative, 9 brings arguments, fire, and sickness associated with the eyes and the heart.

The unlucky numbers

The two numbers to be very wary of in flying star are the numbers 5 and 2. Both these numbers represent the earth element based on the Later Heaven Pa Kua arrangement of trigrams and elements. These two numbers bring grave misfortune and sickness to whoever occupies the palace into which they fly either as the water, mountain, annual, or monthly star. Thus, they should always be strongly resisted and controlled with powerful feng shui cures. These two numbers are said to create the killing energy of sickness similar to, and sometimes more lethal than, those created by physical poison arrows. They cause illness and fatal accidents.

The number 2 is known as a black star, and in the constellation is known as the Huge Door. The number 2 stands for the mother and when it shows its auspicious side, which is during the period of 2, it brings great wealth and prosperity, high positions in the army and is especially benevolent towards women. When it is negative, however, 2 causes the woman to suffer. It can also lead to premature widowhood, miscarriages, serious and fatal illness, and stomach problems.

In the period of seven this number is more deadly than benevolent. To dissolve the bad effects of 2, hang a string of six metal coins at the palace where the number 2 resides. This taps the metal energy of the coin because metal exhausts the earth of 2. The number 6 (hence six coins) represents Chien or big metal in the Pa Kua symbol. The effect of six coins is extremely powerful since 6 also represents the power of heavenly forces. A six-rod windchime is also effective.

The number 5 has a most pernicious effect. This is believed to be the most troublesome of the nine numbers. Five is a yellow number and it is powerful because it is the center number of the original Lo Shu square. Although it is known as the wicked star, nevertheless, in circumstances when it is benevolent, 5 brings exceptional prosperity luck. This occurs during the period of 5. Generally, however, 5 is an unfavorable star number that brings sickness and ill health. To overcome its horrible effects hang a six-rod windchime in the affected palace. This exhausts the energy generated by its earth element. Remember that 5 is at its most harmful when it appears as an annual star (known as the wu wang) or when it is combined with the 9 star. Windchimes are the best way of controlling this star number. The sound of metal caused by windchimes exhausts the earth energy. Another stronger method is to hang a curved knife high up near the ceiling – this symbolically destroys the 5 star.

When both 5 and 2 occur together use a larger windchime to add strength. Alternatively hang six windchimes, or add six coins to make the cure a great deal stronger. Remember that when you hang windchimes they should not hang suspended above anybody's head – so hang them by the side of the wall.

The number 3 is also regarded as an unlucky number. Three is the quarrelsome star that causes misunderstandings, disharmony, and obstacles to manifest. When it is strengthened 3 also brings lawsuits and court cases. In the constellation it is known as the Jade Star and during its own period of 3 it brings wealth and prosperity and benefits the eldest son of the family. However, during periods seven and eight the number 3 is inauspicious and indicates malicious gossip, and injury to the limbs, the hands and legs, fingers and toes. Internally it causes problems with the liver and the bladder. The best way to overcome the negative aspects of 3 is to shine a bright light in the palace where it occurs. Quiet and silent fire energy are also excellent for controlling its pernicious effect. In fact, fire cures for 3 are said to be exceptionally potent. If using bright lights is difficult anything red will work, such as a bright red curtain, or a painting that has predominantly red tones.

The different stars of the natal chart

The lucky or unlucky numbers are placed in the flying star natal chart as either:

1　*The period star*
2　*The water star*
3　*The mountain star*
4　*The annual star*
5　*The monthly star*

When analysis of a flying star chart is attempted we first look at the period star, before moving on to the other stars. All flying star charts display only the first three stars, and these reveal the chi distribution of houses for a period of 20 years. In other words the feng shui influence of the numbers of the first three stars are said to hold true for 20 years, after which their meanings and influence may change. The nature of feng shui, however, is never static and so although we do have 20-year charts nevertheless the luck of houses do not stay the same all through those years. This is where the annual and monthly charts come in. The numbers of the annual and monthly charts exert a heavy influence over the natal chart. Thus for complete analysis of any home it is good practice to also fill in the annual and monthly star numbers. This gives a more complete reading of the chi distribution and luck of any home on a month-by-month basis.

It is also possible to add further inputs in the form of daily Lo Shu charts and hourly Lo Shu charts. When you look into an Almanac you will find that each day also has reigning numbers. And each two-hour segment of the day also has its own reigning Lo Shu number. With this number anyone can generate the full Lo Shu chart, which can then be factored into the natal chart reading.

Example: Here is an example of a natal chart where the year and month have been included. The example used is of a house that faces SW2. We will undertake a simple examination of the luck of this house during May 2003. Note the year 2003 is ruled by the Lo Shu number 6 and in that year, which is the year of the Sheep, the month 6 May to 6 June is ruled by the number 2.

Period 7 House Facing SW2

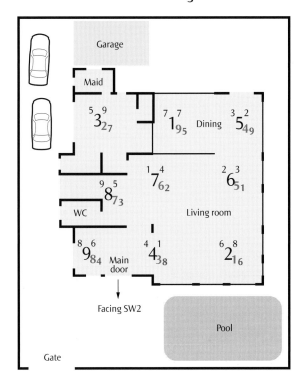

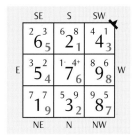

Chi distribution in year 2003

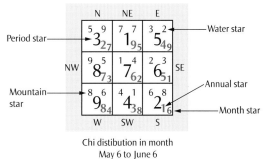

Chi distribution in month
May 6 to June 6

(You can refer to the calendars on page 81 for these two pieces of information.) If you make an attempt to work through this chart and satisfy yourself how each of the numbers in each of the palaces have been placed there you will have come a long way in your mastery of Flying Star feng shui.

The illustration of the period seven house shows the ground level of a bungalow which was massively renovated in 2001. The house has a SW2 orientation and the natal chart was first drawn up as shown in the top chart. The annual numbers for the year 2003 were then added to the chart before it was "turned" so that all the palaces of the chart are oriented in the same direction as the way the layout plan has been drawn. Doing this makes it easy to analyze since all the numbers can be easily superimposed on to a house plan. If you look closely at the numbers of the natal chart itself you will find that the facing palace of this house has the 8 mountain star and the 6 water star. Both numbers are auspicious so the main door is said to be auspicious. In the year 2003 note that the annual number in the facing palace is 8 and this makes 2003 an auspicious year for this house. Next look at its month number – 4. This indicates literary excellence so it is possible that in the month of May, the resident could attain some kind of literary success.

Next look at where the pool is. Note that the natal charts indicate a water star 8 in this corner. This is most auspicious for the wealth luck of this family – especially in the year 2003 when the annual star here is 1, which is also water. The month star meanwhile is 6. So all indications are very positive and I would dare to say that this house will enjoy extreme good fortune in the year 2003. Income luck will be very excellent.

Now lets look at the luck of the less auspicious palaces. Look at the dining room where the natal chart shows the numbers 5, 2, and 3 – all of which are unlucky numbers. The annual number is 4 and the month number is 9. This is not a lucky corner and it is advisable for the family not to eat in that part of the dining room. Instead it is more advantageous to eat in the northeast palace, where the residents will benefit from the double 7 numbers. Both mountain and water stars are 7 so this is very auspicious. However, note that the annual star is 9 and the month star is 5 – so the 5 yellow is strengthened by the annual 9 thereby bringing illness to this house in the month of May. So in this month it is advisable to eat in another part of the house or to eat out. However, note that because of the double 7 stars the 5 here is not very strong.

There is a great deal more which the chart reveals and as we move into more advanced flying star analysis you might want to come back to this example to analyze the numbers as well as the combination of numbers further. Note that when you lay out the floor plan in this way and look closely at the numbers, it is easy to study the chi distribution in the house. This makes it clear how the luck of the house can be tapped. From the chart and layout of this house it is obvious that the owners have taken feng shui advice.

39. STRENGTH OF THE NUMBERS IN DIFFERENT PERIODS

While each of the numbers possesses intrinsic attributes that indicate specific types of good fortune or misfortune, do note that there is a great deal more to this than meets the eye. One of the most important dimensions of numbers analysis in flying star is to factor in the relative strength of the chi of each of the numbers during different periods. There are different levels of chi strength assigned to the numbers as time moves on from period to period.

According to Three Period feng shui (Sarn Yuan feng shui) we can differentiate between six qualities of chi in flying star analysis. These reflect the strength of the numbers and their quality. In each period different numbers represent different types of chi so, irrespective of whether the numbers themselves indicate good fortune or misfortune, it is important to also consider this dimension of the numbers in your analysis. So for period seven we look at the numbers that indicate the strong chi and avoid or "cure" the numbers that represent death and decline. We should do the same for period eight, which is just around the corner. Before summarizing which numbers represent which type of chi let us look at the six types of chi. These are:

Ripening chi This is also known as prosperity, or wang, chi and it is the best energy to tap. When the mountain star is a number that represents wang chi, and it is activated by nearby mountains in the direction indicated by its placement in the chart, those mountains will bring enormous good fortune. When there are no mountains look out for tall buildings that can take the place of mountains. When there are no tall buildings, hang a painting of mountains in the palace which has this auspicious mountain star and watch your fortunes improve by leaps and bounds. This is because the meaning of this kind of chi is that "your luck has ripened, it has arrived."

In the same way, when the water star of any sector has the number which indicates ripening chi of that period it suggests the potential for great wealth to arrive very quickly. The chi has to be activated by the presence of real water, and the water should be Yang water – it should be moving, clean and, better yet, have some fish swimming in it. There is really no better energizer than alive water. Note that in the period of seven the number which represents ripening chi is the number 7 itself. In any period it is the number of the period that represents the ripening chi. So in the period of eight the number that represents ripening chi is the number 8.

Growing chi This is also referred to as Sheng chi – this is energy that is growing stronger, expanding, about to blossom. This number possesses chi that signifies coming good fortune. This can mean a whole variety of things: promotion at work, upward mobility in one's career, a major political appointment, an offer you cannot refuse, anything at all that can qualify as making progress. In business it can suggest getting a major infusion of cash, an attractive takeover offer, or a major new contract. When the mountain star has this number it means that recognition is just round the corner. When the water star has this number it means a windfall is about to come your way. But for these things to happen both the mountain and water star must be activated.

In the period of seven the number which represents Sheng chi is the number 8, as this indicates coming prosperity. In the period of eight the number that signifies Sheng chi is the number 9, so look out for these two numbers and make sure you activate them correctly in the palaces where they occur.

Improving chi This is the number which indicates that luck is improving because all the obstacles confronting you are weakening. Luck has not arrived but there will be signs of improvement. This number should not be energized – this is because the energy of this number is weak and activating it will only cause it to retreat. So improving chi numbers should be left alone. The number that represents improving chi in the period of seven is the number 9, and in the period of eight it is number 1. This kind of chi is akin to distant prosperity. It is a very long term type of good energy.

Declining chi This is the number which suggest that luck is waning, energy is weakening, and obstacles to success are piling up. Luck is slipping away. When the mountain star has this number it indicates that power and influence are definitely on the decline. Those who do not want to lose their positions in high office must make very sure they do not stay in a room where the mountain star shows this number. Similarly those in business who are going through hard times must make sure they do not stay in a room where the water star shows this number if they want their companies to survive. And they should not live in a house where the water star at the facing palace has this number. Declining fortunes are truly painful to experience so do take strong precautions. In the period of seven the number which signifies declining chi is 6 and in the period of eight it is 7.

Dead chi This is the number that suggests danger and decay. It is also known as Si chi. Various manifestations of bad luck are visited upon those affected by the numbers signifying dead chi. There is no more life and no more progress. The energy has simply died. It is necessary to try to move out of rooms afflicted by dead chi numbers (manifested as either water or mountain stars). Alternatively, the number can be brought to life again! You can do this by using the element cycles. Thus in the period of seven the numbers that signify dead chi are 1 and 4. To bring the number 1 to life again you will need to rejuvenate it with metal, so placing coins in the sector will do wonders to revive the chi of the number. To bring the 4 to life you will need water. However, when energizing dead chi numbers it is necessary to guard against overdoing things. Moderation is important with this particular cure.

The dead chi numbers in the period of eight are the numbers 4 and 6. Once again, to bring these numbers to life use the productive cycle of the five elements. So use earth, for instance boulders and crystals, to revive the number 6.

Killing chi This is Shar chi – the most powerfully destructive chi. It is necessary to watch out for these harmful star numbers. When the mountain star is this number, which represents Shar chi in the current period, it causes residents to suffer from sudden and violent death. Other manifestations are being a victim of murder, sickness, or suicide. The numbers that signify killing chi in the period of seven are the numbers 2, 3, and 5. As these are intrinsically very unlucky and troublesome numbers anyway it is necessary to be ever watchful about where these numbers appear. It is vital to use feng shui cures that can press down and at least control these numbers. The best way to suppress the killing energy of 2 and 5 is to use metal windchimes and the best way to suppress the killing energy of 3 is to use the color red. But it should be a red that is Yin, i.e. silent, so red curtains, red paintings, or red lights would do the job very well. Because 3 is also the quarrelsome star it is important not to activate it with noise and moving objects. In the period of eight the killing chi numbers are also 2, 3, and 5 so the same cures will apply.

Table of chi energy of the numbers 1 to 9 in the nine periods

PERIOD	UPPER	UPPER	UPPER	MIDDLE	MIDDLE	MIDDLE	LOWER	LOWER	LOWER
PERIOD	1	2	3	4	5	6	7	8	9
RIPENING	1	2	3	4	5	6	7	8	9
GROWING	2	3	4	5	6	7	8	9	1
IMPROVING	3	4	5	6	7	8	9	1	2
DECLINING	9	1	2	3	4	5	6	7	8
DEAD	6, 7	9, 6	1, 6	2, 8	2, 3	4, 9	1, 4	4, 6	4, 6
KILLING	5, 7	5, 7	7	2, 7	2, 3	2, 3	2, 3, 5	2, 3, 5	3, 5, 7

The nine cycles of chi

The information contained in the table above, which shows the chi energy of the numbers in different periods, is very similar to the nine cycles of chi as manifested in houses built in different periods. The nine cycles of chi looks at the different period houses and assigns different strengths to their chi. This takes account of the chi of any house. This is one of the most closely-guarded secrets in the application of Flying Star feng shui. When you study how the chi of houses waxes and wanes from period to period you will realize that the chi of houses can and does get exhausted unless it is properly re-energized.

How is this done? How can we bring new life to old houses that suffer from exhausted chi? It is obvious that when the chi of any abode is tired or even dead, the residents will be adversely affected.

The secret of flying star is that chi must always be replenished. This is what gives strength to one's good fortune; this is what sustains family fortunes. When the chi of the family abode is regularly revitalized family fortunes stay intact and even expand from one generation to the next. When the chi of family homes is allowed to dwindle and die, the fortunes of the family also get dispersed. Descendants lose their close ties to the family.

Revitalizing chi means making sure the house is always well-maintained and kept in good condition. Everything in the house should work, from the plumbing to the electricity. Bulbs are never left unchanged and there are no wilting flowers left in vases. Revitalizing also means replenishing Yang energy to keep the house chi alive and active. When abandoned and left to rot, houses literally die, Yang energy seeps out, wilts, and then the energy of the house grows Yin until finally it goes to sleep completely!

So even if you do not know flying star, if you frequently introduce movement, change, redecorate, do small renovations to your home, this alone revitalizes it and brings in fresh strong chi that can only benefit residents. This is good feng shui – good for health and for bringing opportunities in all areas of your life. It is for this reason that I always do something with my home every year. And also why I hold a Chinese New Year party each year – to bring in precious Yang chi that keeps my home bustling with happiness and good health. Knowing flying star enables me to make certain I keep all auspicious flying stars nicely activated, and all bad stars under control. This is why I enjoy feng shui so much, and this is what I am trying so hard to pass on to my readers – not simply the knowledge and the methodology of feng shui but also, more importantly, a positive attitude towards its practice. Harmony in the home can do with a helping hand from feng shui but one's attitude must also be positive.

Be careful, however, never to become obsessive or dogmatic in the practice of feng shui. The moment you get up-tight about feng shui, or allow some so-called master to scare you, is when all the fun is taken out of feng shui – and then it gets into a negative spiral. All the true and genuine feng shui masters I have ever met (and believe me, I have met many) are always full of good humor, and are extremely humble and understated. They never ever criticize other practitioners. From them I have learnt a good deal more than feng shui!

The tips summarized here offer practical references based on the nine cycles of chi. From these tips you will be able to get a feel for houses built in different periods.

1   *Houses built during periods one, six, and eight have strong chi, while houses built during periods two and five tend to be weak. This means that period one, six, and eight houses enjoy good chi in many other periods. Period two and five houses tend to have weak, dead chi in most other periods. So if you purchase a house built in period two or five go all out to revitalize its chi and change its period by undertaking large-scale renovations – lots of banging and knocking.*

2 *The chi of all houses declines in the period that comes immediately after the period in which they were built. Thus all period seven houses will suffer a massive decline in energy, a serious weakening, from 4 February 2004 onwards, because this is the day when period seven becomes period eight.*

3 *In period seven, all houses built in periods one, four, five, and nine have dead energy. Houses built in period six have declining energy.*

4 *In period eight, no houses except period seven houses suffer from dead energy. Houses built in periods one, two, three, four, five, and six enjoy good energy. Only period seven houses suffer from declining energy and it is for this reason that I am strongly recommending that everyone presently living in a period seven house changes the period of their house into a period eight house. In fact this is the prime motivation for my writing this advanced book of feng shui. Unless you change the period of your house, the probability of you suffering severe misfortunes after 2004 is very high.*

40. FLYING STAR COMBINATIONS WITH ENHANCERS AND CURES

More important than understanding single numbers is the correct interpretation of combinations of numbers. When I say "combination of numbers" I am referring to the following combinations:

- *Combinations of mountain star with water star*
- *Combinations of period star with mountain star*
- *Combinations of period star with water star*
- *Combinations of annual and month stars with natal chart stars*

Different flying star practitioners place different emphasis on these combinations. You will find that there are those who look only at the mountain and water stars. They tend to downplay the importance of the period star; their argument being that no one's luck can be consistently good or bad for as long as 20 years. So to them it is the water stars and mountains stars and how these react to the annual and month stars that give a really true picture of chi strength and distribution in any house.

Equally as many masters look at the period and water, as well as the period and mountain combinations. This group considers it ridiculous that the period stars are ignored, and I tend to agree. In my analysis of flying star charts I study all aspects and all dimensions and try to then take a holistic view of what the numbers are telling me. Sometimes I find that certain combinations of numbers just jump up at me, especially when the surrounding environment – the roads and mountains, buildings and rivers – all point to exciting feng shui potential. At other times, because I am searching for specific manifestations of bad combinations to explain why a friend or a family is having a spate of bad luck, I look to find what I am searching for.

So I prefer to adopt a less dogmatic approach, preferring to keep an open mind and allowing for a certain amount of flexibility of possibilities. I do urge you to do the same. It is really beneficial to remember that feng shui is an ancient practice which we are trying to transplant into a thoroughly modern environment. So do allow for the fact that interpretations of the numbers in terms of aspirations and even definitions of success, happiness, love, and so forth will have different connotations today than they did a thousand years ago in China!

In terms of just looking at the numbers, perhaps the best starting point is to look out for some of the important combinations. These are summarized here under auspicious and inauspicious combinations.

Auspicious combinations to look out for

Firstly there are the combinations that spell wealth luck. These are indicated by the auspicious white numbers 1, 6, and 8 occurring together in a single palace. The main star, water star, and mountain star make up this combination of numbers. Of all the stars the white ones are always the most auspicious and in the Lower Period, i.e. in the present period, the number 8 is the major white star. The number 1 is the supporting star while the number 6 is the declining white star. This gives you an idea of the strength of their chi. Note, therefore, how incredibly important the number 8 is in the current and next period that lasts until 2043.

Secondly there is a combination that indicates the potential for marriage, the birth of a child, or a celebration of a family member's longevity. These events are collectively referred to as happiness occasions or, in Chinese, hei see. When the bedroom or the main door is located in a palace with the combination of 4 and 1, with the 4 being the mountain star and the 1 being the water star, it indicates happiness occasions. In modern-day feng shui such occasions can also be extended to include college graduation, as well as the son or daughter of the family starting out on their career.

Next there are the doubles: the double 7 in the period of seven charts and the double 8 in the period of eight charts. For now it is the double 7 that engages us, since the beneficial effect of this combination (if you have it in the natal chart of your home) can still be felt until 4 February 2004. Even though the chi of 7 has already started to weaken, nevertheless while we are in the period of seven the double 7 remains auspicious. This combination refers to the mountain and water stars both being 7. It is best when the double 7 is at the facing palace where the main door is located or at the back door. To activate this combination, place water near the door and have a view of a mountain further away. This way you capture both the mountain and water. If the mountain is too near i.e. if there is a wall near to the entrance and there is also water nearby, then the mountain is said to have fallen into the water. This situation means that the residents will become rich but they could also lose their good name, their health, or their popularity. Doubles, either in front or behind, always benefit from the presence of real water and real mountains.

Below are some additional meanings to the combinations of the main star with the water star. Unless stated otherwise, these are auspicious when present in all the palaces. Note the first number is the main number and the second number is the water star number.

- *1/4 or 4/1 mean success in examinations and scholarly pursuits. Rooms with such combinations should be given to your college-going children*
- *6/8 means success in business, while 8/6 means scholarly pursuits*
- *4/6 means talent and fame*
- *8/9 means a happy family with lots of happiness occasions*
- *9/8 means fame*
- *2/8 in the northwest means great wealth*
- *3/1 in the west means many descendants*
- *Combinations of 1/6, 1/1, 1/8, 6/4, 6/6, and 8/8 all mean good fortune and great health. In the central palace, also known as the heavenly heart, these numbers benefit the whole family. Interactions in specific rooms affect activities in those rooms and benefit those residing there.*

There are also other special combinations that suggest auspicious potential, especially when properly activated. These "specials" take us deeper into flying star interpretations and I have included them all in the next chapter. These advanced readings include the four sets of Ho Tu numbers, the three sets of the parent string numbers, and so forth. Other combinations take account of the flight path of the stars and the strength of Yin and Yang of the numbers. For the moment it is sufficient to attain a certain familiarity with the common combinations first. These are easy to spot and easy to activate. They bring very fast results and this should inspire you to move on to the next level of learning.

Combinations that spell danger and discord

Firstly there is the combination that indicates severe illness, loss, accidents, and misfortunes. This is the combination of the star numbers 2 and 5, especially when they are the mountain and water stars. When the combination involves a main star the effect of the 5 is said to be lessened marginally. When the mountain star is 5 it indicates loss of a loved one, an important friend, or loss of a job. When the mountain star is 2 it indicates severe illness, hospitalization, contracting a disease, having an operation etc. When the water star is 5 it indicates a loss of wealth, declining profits, and severe financial problems. When the water star is 2 it suggests mental illness, succumbing to pressure, and an inability to cope with finances. These two numbers are indeed to be feared, and they create enormous mischief for residents when they fly into the facing palace. This is the palace that houses the main front door into the home. They also cause problems when they are inside your bedroom.

The impact of the 2 and 5 become more fatal when the annual 5 or annual 2 also fly in to strengthen the combination. I simply cannot over emphasize the danger of such a situation. The impact of the 5s or 2s all congregated in one palace is like having a bomb in there! The best way to cope with the 5/2 disastrous combination is simply to move out of any room occupied by these numbers. Use that room as a storeroom, because this way you are imprisoning the bad stars. Locking them up, I have discovered, is an excellent way of coping with these horrible stars.

Another excellent cure I find very effective is, of course, metal windchimes. These are able to exhaust the afflicted chi of the 5 and the 2. Metal coins placed in a row above doorways is also favored by flying star experts from Hong Kong. Indeed in Hong Kong many of the homes of the local tycoons also have depictions of mountains that are made of metal. These are said to be most effective in keeping the 2 and 5 under wraps.

Secondly, there is also danger indicated when you encounter the troublesome doubles i.e. the double 5s and double 2s. These can easily extend into triples when we factor in the annual and monthly stars, so do strenuously avoid the doubles. The combination can be the main star with either the water or mountain star, or it could be water and mountain. It is vital to use the windchime or coin cure to exhaust the energy of the double 2s and 5s. If one sleeps or works in a place that is afflicted by these numbers, the 2s will bring severe even fatal sickness while the 5s will bring loss or accidents.

Thirdly there is the combination of 3/2 or 2/3. This is a quarrelsome combination and wherever it is present it sows discord and dissent. This is a combination that simply must not be activated by noise or activity. The more the combination gets activated the greater the likelihood of residents encountering problems with the authorities, with bureaucracy, and with the courts. Litigation could engage the residents and there will be a great deal of disharmony. The best way to overcome the energy of the 3/2 combination is to use the color red, but it must be a silent red – for instance, a red lamp. The red exhausts the 3 without activating it. Some practitioners do not like using red because they say it strengthens the sickness star 2, since fire makes earth in the element cycle but I have discovered that red always works. Two other cures I have used with great success are solid crystal balls and Yin water. Place six round crystal balls in the afflicted palace to promote harmony. Alternatively, place an urn or a big vase filled with non-moving water. The Chinese word for vase is ping, and this also means peace. That is why the Chinese are so fond of ceramic vases. In any sector they signify harmony of relations. When you have the 3 present, at all costs avoid hanging windchimes, clocks, or other moving objects. Also do not place the radio or television there as this will only activate the 3.

Next we need to consider the combination of 5/9 or 9/5 . This is a combination that represents a very much strengthened 5. The fire energy of 9 magnifies the fatal earth energy of 5 and, where it occurs, this combination creates severe blocks to success. It can also cause accidents that lead to fairly serious injury. The best way to control this combination is by using metal windchimes. You will need six-rod windchimes for this since we require the added boost of metal represented by the number six.

Here is a summary of inauspicious combinations in a natal chart. The meanings apply to all the palaces. Note that the first number refers to the mountain star while the second number refers to the water star.

- *7/9 indicates problems caused by political intrigues. Use Yin water in a vase to overcome*
- *2/5 or 5/2 means severe illness. Use windchimes to overcome*
- *3/7 mean loss of fortunes through robbery or legal hassle. Use Yin fire energy – red cloth, lamp etc*
- *9/7 means fire caused by human activity. Control with Yin water in a vase*
- *2/7 means fire caused by natural occurrence. Use Yin water in a vase*
- *5/5 means severe illness. Control with metal windchimes*
- *5/9 means accidents leading to hospitalization or death. Use windchimes*
- *7/6 or 6/7 means armed robbery leading to injury. Use Yin water in a vase to control*
- *7/3 means betrayal, trickery, and intrigue at work. Be careful. Use lights to overcome*
- *3/7 means illness caused by worry and anxieties. Victim of politics. Use lights*
- *6/9 means illness of internal organs. Older residents at risk. Place wu lou in the room*
- *8/4 or 3/8 means unhealthy children always sick. Use six coins placed over entrance*
- *2/9 means obstacles in business ventures. Use metal bells to overcome*
- *2/3 indicates too many mouths to feed. Use Yin water in a vase*

Combinations of numbers in a natal chart

Here are some more meanings to work with. Not all the combinations given here are equally important. They are nevertheless included, in case you need to analyze houses from other periods. Before studying more on the meanings of number combinations it is useful once again to familiarize yourself with a natal chart. On the following page is the natal chart of a house that faces the direction S1. See how much of this you are already familiar with.

Revision and reminders

1   *The combinations of all the numbers inside the nine palaces are important. The little numbers on the left and right of the big central number are known as the mountain star (on the left) and the water star (on the right). These numbers indicate relationship and wealth luck respectively.*
2   *Note that auspicious water stars can be activated by physical water while auspicious mountain stars are enhanced by physical hills and mountains.*

South 1

This number is the annual number and it indicates the luck for the year 2002

SE	S	SW
2 3 **6** 6	7 7 **2** 2	9 5 **4** 4
1 4 **5** 5	3 2 **7** 7	5 9 **9** 9
6 8 **1** 1	8 6 **3** 3	4 1 **8** 8
NE	N	NW

E ... W

The big number is the period star, also known as the main star number

This little number is the mountain star, which indicates the luck of relationships

This little number on the right is the water star, which represents money luck

3 Note the elements of the numbers. Remember that these elements are based on the trigram placement of the Later Heaven arrangement of the Pa Kua. Thus 1 is water, 2 is earth, 3 is wood, 4 is wood, 5 is earth, 6 is metal, 7 is metal, 8 is earth, and 9 is fire. Take note of these number/element combinations and commit them to memory if you wish to become a feng shui practitioner.

4 Each of the directions has an element. Thus north is water, southwest is earth, southeast is wood, east is wood, the center is earth, northwest is metal, west is metal, northeast is earth, and south is fire. When a number flies into a corner always think "which element is flying into which element" and then ask yourself if the incoming element is enhancing, exhausting, or destroying the element of the palace or sector. This alone offers instant clues on whether the number flying into any sector is good or bad.

5 The result or outcome of numbers coming into a sector can be auspicious or inauspicious. If they are inauspicious they can always be corrected. How? With the correct use of element analysis.

6 The combinations of water and mountain stars can be analyzed to indicate if they are auspicious or inauspicious. How good your feng shui analysis will be depends on your judgment of what kind of cures should be used.

7 Never forget the impact of the time stars. Each hour, day, month, year, and each 20-year period has different reigning Lo Shu numbers that can be expanded into charts. These time stars exert their influence on the palaces. When there is a concentration of bad stars on a particular day or month, any negative or positive effect is considerably strengthened. Based on this, combinations are never always good and seldom always bad. It depends on other stars combining with them.

8 *Finally, when bad stars or good stars combine they often need a catalyst – an external feature or structure – to trigger an effect. It's a bit like karma ripening at a particular moment in time. Thus external forms and structures combine with flying stars to speed up good and bad effects. Similarly, symbolic decorative pieces have the same triggering effect. So when a bad annual star flies into a sector with unlucky natal chart numbers, bad luck gets triggered much faster when that affected palace is also being hurt by a poison arrow.*

The table on the following pages gives the meaning of combinations of water and mountain star numbers. This table is similar to the earlier table of trigram and annual number combinations, but there are instances where the combinations yield slightly different meanings. Therefore do not use the two tables interchangeably.

Table of Meanings of Combinations of Numbers

MOUNTAIN STAR	WATER STAR	INDICATED DIVINATIONS AND OUTCOMES OF THE COMBINATION	ENHANCERS FOR GOOD LUCK COMBINATIONS OR REMEDIES FOR BAD LUCK COMBINATIONS
1	2	Marriage problems and danger of losses. Water in mountain is a sign of grave danger, just as mountain falling into water is a very bad sign indeed	Use plants to exhaust the water and strengthen earth element
2	1	The matriarch is too strong leading to marital problems	Use metal to exhaust
1	3	Wealth and fame luck are indicated	Use water to enhance and water plants
3	1	Prosperity luck is so good, if you don't have the karma/luck to live in this home you will change residence	Plant a bamboo grove to strengthen your luck
1	4	Political luck. Media and publicity luck. Romance luck	Use slow-moving water but not too much
4	1	Romance luck but too much water leads to sex scandals. Affairs leading to unhappiness and breakup of family	Use plant to strengthen wood
1	5	Health problems relating to the kidneys	Use a windchime
5	1	Hearing problems and sex-related illness	Use a windchime
1	6	Auspicious. Intelligence with great commercial skills	Enhance with metal
6	1	Financial luck and high achievers in the family	Enhance with metal
1	7	Good money luck in period of 7 only, in period of 8 this combination means loss of wealth	Enhance with crystals or gem tree
7	1	Extremely good prosperity luck	Use water feature
1	8	Excellent wealth luck into period 8	Enhance with crystals

MOUNTAIN STAR	WATER STAR	INDICATED DIVINATIONS AND OUTCOMES OF THE COMBINATION	ENHANCERS FOR GOOD LUCK COMBINATIONS OR REMEDIES FOR BAD LUCK COMBINATIONS
8	1	Excellent and auspicious luck. Money and family luck	Enhance with water
1	9	Good combination but can turn bad when 5 flies in	Do not enhance
9	1	Same as above	Do not disturb
2	3	Arguments and misunderstandings of the most severe kind. Back stabbing, hatred, legal disputes. Inauspicious	Use still water to cool tempers. Do not disturb
3	2	As bad as above and can get dangerous for those in politics. Tendency to obesity	Some masters recommend gold and fire
2	4	Wives and mothers-in-law quarrel and fight. Disharmony	Use water
4	2	Illness of internal organs. Husband has affairs	Use water
2	5	Extremely inauspicious. Total loss and catastrophe. This is one of the most dangerous combinations in Flying Star technology, and when the 5 flies in, anyone staying here could suddenly have an accident or develop terminal illness	Use windchime (plenty). Beware – do not have fire or could result in death
5	2	Misfortunes and extreme bad luck. Illness may be fatal	Use windchime
2	6	Very easy life of ease and leisure. This auspicious combination is spoilt if a five-rod windchime is placed here. The trinity (tien ti ren) gets activated in a negative way	Do not spoil the luck here with windchimes. Said to attract earth spirits!
6	2	Great affluence and everything successful	No need to enhance

MOUNTAIN STAR	WATER STAR	INDICATED DIVINATIONS AND OUTCOMES OF THE COMBINATION	ENHANCERS FOR GOOD LUCK COMBINATIONS OR REMEDIES FOR BAD LUCK COMBINATIONS
2	7	There is richness and money during the period of 7 but luck of children will not be good. Problems conceiving children. Period of 8 everything is bad!	Use metal (bells) in period of 7 and water in period of 8
7	2	Money luck dissipates. Children luck is dimmed	Use windchimes
2	8	Richness and wealth but there is ill health, although this is minor and can be remedied	Use water to overcome bad health star
8	2	Better than above. There is money luck	Use mountain principle
2	9	Extremely bad luck. Nothing succeeds unless remedied	Use water plants
9	2	Better luck than above	Use water
3	4	Danger of mental instability. Tendency to stress	Use bright lights
4	3	Emotional stress due to relationship problems	Use red to overcome
3	5	Loss of wealth. Severe cash flow problems. If bedroom is here, financial loss is severe. If kitchen is here sickness is inevitable. Better not to stay in this part of the house	Exhaust the 5 with metal but not with windchimes or bells. Use copper mountain painting
5	3	Money troubles. Disputes. Bad business luck	Use Yin water
3	6	Period of slow growth	Use Yin water
6	3	Unexpected windfall. Speculative luck	Enhance with gemstones
3	7	You will get robbed or burgled. Violence. Not so bad in period of 7 but sure to get robbed in period of 8	Use Yin water

MOUNTAIN STAR	WATER STAR	INDICATED DIVINATIONS AND OUTCOMES OF THE COMBINATION	ENHANCERS FOR GOOD LUCK COMBINATIONS OR REMEDIES FOR BAD LUCK COMBINATIONS
7	3	Grave danger of injury to limbs. Be careful	Use Yin water
3	8	Not good for children under 12 years	Use bright lights to cure
8	3	Move children away from this sector	Use red and yellow
4	5	Prone to sexually-transmitted diseases. Breast cancer	Use water/mountain
5	4	Just as bad as above	Use water/mountain
4	6	Bad luck for women who will bear heavy burden	Strengthen earth element
6	4	Unexpected windfall for women	Enhance with windchime
4	7	Bad luck in love. Will get cheated by opposite sex	Use Yang water
7	4	Taken for a ride by someone of the opposite sex	Use Yang water
4	8	Bad for very young children	Use lights to combat
8	4	Overpowering matriarch. Love lives of younger generation will suffer from the wiles of the mother	Use fire or red to overcome
4	9	A time for preparation. Good for students	Use wood or plants
9	4	Good luck for those starting new business	Use water to enhance
5/7	7/5	Problems caused by excessive gossiping. Danger of poisoning or anything to do with the mouth	Use metal in period of 7 and water in period of 8
5/8	8/5	Problems related to the limbs, joints, and bones of the body. It is necessary to be wary of rough sports	Use Yin water to pacify
5/9	9/5	Bad luck and tempers. Excessive mental disorder or stress – there is unhappiness and dissatisfaction	Use windchime Water/mountain theory

MOUNTAIN STAR	WATER STAR	INDICATED DIVINATIONS AND OUTCOMES OF THE COMBINATION	ENHANCERS FOR GOOD LUCK COMBINATIONS OR REMEDIES FOR BAD LUCK COMBINATIONS
6/7	7/6	Negative chi "sword fighting killing breath"	Use Yin water
6/8	8/6	Wealth, popularity, prosperity. Great richness. Probably the best combination in Flying Star technique	Enhance with water and make sure you have an entrance or window in that sector
7/9	9/7	Extreme problems during period of 8. All troubles will be caused through excessive vulnerability to sexual advances. There is also danger of fire	Use water or earth (big boulders) to press down on the bad luck

The use of remedies to overcome flying star afflictions

1. *To correct financial problems focus your remedy on the water star (siang sin – the facing star). If the water star is auspicious, enhance it with water. If the water star is bad or unlucky, exhaust it with wood.*

2. *To correct health and relationship matters focus on the mountain star (chor sin – the sitting star). When the mountain star is auspicious, enhance with crystals. And when the mountain star is unlucky or bad, exhaust it with water. Let the mountain symbolically "fall into the water" and its bad effects will be instantly rectified. Water here can simply mean a hole in the ground.*

3. *To improve your feng shui readings and investigations, never forget the annual flying star afflictions – the Grand Duke, the Three Killings, and the Five Yellow.*

4. *Always look at the structures, levels, and roads in the landscape that could trigger the bad numbers. When the landscape is bad, i.e. when there are poison arrows in the form of a directly-hitting straight road, a triangular roof line, or a transmission tower, these act as catalysts for bad luck to manifest quickly.*

41. NINE PALACES OF THE HOME

Now that you have developed familiarity with the flying star natal chart, we need to move on to address the practical aspects of using flying star. It is not necessary to analyze the luck of every little corner of the home. As long as the auspicious numbers are in the palaces of the chart that fall into the important sectors of the home, the feng shui will be incredibly good. Good feng shui practice ensures this. All natal charts have good and bad palaces, potentially excellent and potentially dangerous palaces. How these palaces are captured, activated, or imprisoned is at the heart of real feng shui. When you get the arrangement of your house layout correct from this perspective your feng shui will bring you enormous good fortune.

Not all the rooms in the home have equal importance, so let's look at the most crucial areas.

The facing palace

The most important part of any house in terms of getting the flying star right is what we term the facing palace. Generally this is the sector of the house where the main door is located. Sometimes it may not be where the main door is located but instead be on the other side of the house facing, for instance, a beautiful view of a valley. In such a cases, the facing palace is at once at a disadvantage simply because without a main door there it doesn't get activated. When there is a door in the facing palace each time people move in and out of the house the palace is getting activated and if there are auspicious numbers there, the potential for good fortune gets energized.

Sometimes there may be a door in the facing palace but the door may be facing a different direction from the house orientation. This is fine as long as the natal chart was drawn up based on the house facing orientation rather than the door facing direction.

There are many special cures that refer directly to the facing palace under advanced feng shui readings in the next chapter. Many of these call for the placement of water near the vicinity of the facing palace, as this is one of the best ways of energizing this important palace of the home. I have included a special section on water but for now note that water must be on the left-hand side of the main front door. This means looking out the water should be on the left. This guideline holds true irrespective of whether the water is inside or outside the house. Note that water placed on the right can result in the man of the house falling prey to predatory females outside of the marriage.

The palace of the master bedroom

The second most important palace is the master bedroom. It is really worthwhile going out of your way to sleep in the palace that hosts the most auspicious mountain as well as water stars. If you have to choose between the two, pick the palace with the most auspicious water star. This could be 7 or 8 in the period of seven and is definitely the water star 8 in the period of eight. There is no need to activate with water in the bedroom and indeed it is not advisable to do so. Usually bedrooms are placed on the upper levels of homes so it is sufficient to activate the lower level of this palace. If you cannot get the water star 8 for whatever reason then select other auspicious white stars. Number 1 should be the second choice, while 6 would come a distant third. This is because 6 is a tired old star in period seven – but 6 would be much better than sleeping in a place with the dangerous 5s or 2s.

Corridors and staircases

Contrary to what many amateur feng shui enthusiasts think, the corridors and staircases of homes are really important places and they benefit from having auspicious star numbers. Although no one stays in a corridor or a staircase nevertheless these are conduits of chi. The energy of a home flows from room to room through these corridors. Staircases should therefore have auspicious numbers.

Converting the central palace into a cell

A novel but effective method of overcoming the pernicious influence of bad stars like the 5s, the 2s, and the 3s is to literally lock them up inside specially constructed "cells." A storeroom, for instance, can be used to imprison troublesome stars so the household does not feel their malevolence. The size of the storeroom is unimportant it should simply be kept locked and undisturbed. This is one of the more effective ways of taking care of the Five Yellow.

This method is strongly recommended by some of the more experienced masters to control an afflicted central palace. This occurs when the central grid of the house, which is also known as the heart palace, is seriously afflicted with the dangerous 5 star. In the period of seven all east-facing houses have 5 as the water star in the center of the house, and this causes the house to become afflicted by what is known as the "hidden alarm bell warning of danger." A west-facing house has the 5 as the mountain star and this too is equally dangerous. The center of the house is said to designate the throne, the seat of power. This is the sun and the moon, heaven and the earth meeting, the essence of Yin and Yang. The chi of houses converges in the central part of the house. Thus when bad stars fly into the center of the house it is a good idea to keep them locked up by having a small room in the center.

In the house shown below, the 5 mountain star in the heart palace is effectively imprisoned in a cell. However, the 5/2 in the dining room must be controlled with windchimes. The 2/5 in the garage does no harm.

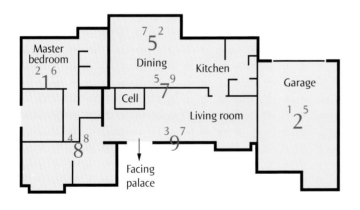

Period 7 House Facing West 2

SE	S	SW
6 1 6	1 5 2	8 3 4
7 2 5	5- 9- 7	3 7 9
2 6 1	9 4 3	4 8 8

E ... W

NE — N — NW

Chart turned to facilitate analysis

NE	E	SE
2 6 1	7 2 5	6 1 6
9 4 3	5 9 7	1 5 2
4 8 8	3 7 9	8 3 4

N ... S

NW — W — SW

Spreading auspicious stars of the heart palace

On the other hand, when the center water and mountain stars are auspicious, such as when the number 8 flies in either as water or mountain star e.g. in houses that have a facing direction of northwest or southeast, then the feng shui thing to do would be to knock down the walls that imprison these auspicious stars. Creating an open hall would be a smart thing to do since this in effect spreads the auspicious influence to the rest of the house. Good fortune chi then gets distributed to a greater floor area of the house. This is what I have done to capture the good fortune chi for this whole period of seven. The star numbers in my heart palace are extremely auspicious so I had all the walls separating the living and the dining rooms taken down. What I have now is a big open space, a bright hall that benefits from the benevolent stars.

Illustrated here is a floor plan showing how this has been done in this apartment, which has a northwest-facing flying star chart. This means that this apartment is located in a building that is oriented northwest. So note that for apartments you should cast the natal chart according to

Period 7 Apartment in a NW-Facing Apartment Block

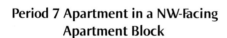

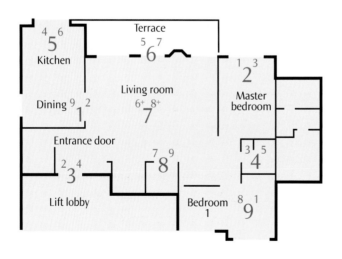

the facing orientation of the whole building and not based on the entrance to the apartment unit. This is an important point to note. The natal chart is then superimposed onto the floor plan of this apartment according to compass directions. Note, however, that the facing palace of the apartment is not located in the northwest palace but is in the north palace instead. Here the numbers are not great – the 4 is a dead star in period seven and 2 brings illness. The numbers in the south sector are not auspicious either. However, the biggest area of the apartment, the living area, benefits from good stars.

Later in advanced feng shui you will see that there are other even more auspicious numbers that can occupy the heart palace. If you are fortunate enough to have such a configuration of numbers it is worth seriously considering enlarging the space of the center of your home, be it an apartment or a bungalow. This not only taps the good numbers for a large floor area but also creates a bright hall, a physical feature that brings a great deal of good fortune. The feeling of space also allows benevolent chi to settle and if you also have a terrace (as in the apartment here) it draws in extra bright chi from the great outdoors.

Residents should occupy palaces according to their Kua numbers

Residents who occupy any of the palaces are said to bring with them their own intrinsic chi as defined by their Kua number. The formula for obtaining one's Kua numbers based on the Eight Mansions School of feng shui has already been covered. From the Kua number can be derived your self, or personal, element as well as your self number, which can now be used in conjunction with Flying Star feng shui to select the most auspicious room for you. According to the texts, residents exert vital chi presence and when their chi harmonizes with that of the home, good fortune will abound. The method of analyzing if a room is good for you is very easy.

Simply check if the mountain star or water star empowers and produces your Kua number. For instance, if your Kua number is 2 you belong to the earth element. If the room you occupy has the double 7, you will see instantly that although the double 7 is most auspicious nevertheless the metal of 7 will exhaust the earth of 2. So you will forever feel tired and tense even though your projects are successful. However, if the Kua 2 person lived in a room with the 5/9 combination of stars then, even though the 5/9 is not a desirable combination, the harmony between 5 and 2 (both being earth numbers) and between 2 and 9 (here the fire of 9 produces the earth of 2) makes this an excellent room for them. Study the following illustration of an apartment shared by two brothers. Paul and Roger used to occupy rooms that had flying star numbers that clashed with their respective Kua numbers. Roger (Kua 2) occupied bedroom 2, where the metal of the 7s exhausted him terribly, leaving him constantly tired. Paul (Kua 1) used to occupy bedroom 1 where the fire chi clashed with his water, while the earth chi destroyed his earth chi. He could not find employment and success eluded him. The answer was for them to switch rooms. Having done so, Paul is presently doing well as an investment banker while Roger has an expanding business. Both brothers are thus flourishing.

So the clever way to apply this small but important guideline is to see how your Kua element interacts with the respective elements of the water and mountain stars. If the water star element produces your Kua element then obviously money luck for you will be excellent. And if the mountain star element produces your element then your popularity, health, and social life will be most fortunate. In contrast, if the water star number element destroys your Kua element then sleeping there will cause you to lose money. If it is the mountain star number that destroys your Kua number element then sleeping in that palace will cause you to lose power, authority, and influence.

Two Brothers Living in a NW3-facing Apartment

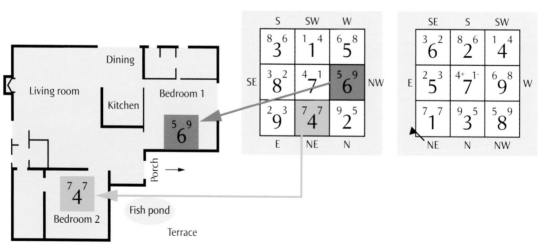

Important reminders in analyzing flying star charts

When analyzing flying star charts please always note that every combination of star numbers can have good as well as bad outcomes. The outcomes depend on these four factors:

1 *Whether or not the numbers have been effectively activated with elements or symbols that magnify their energy.*
2 *Whether or not the numbers are in their positive or negative period cycle – this means how strong their chi is, as well as the quality of their chi in the current period. Remember that numbers have different strengths in different periods.*
3 *Whether or not the element of the incoming stars (i.e. the water and mountain stars) strengthen or weaken the palace they occupy. There are remedies for bad stars and energizers for good stars and these are usually based on the application of the element cycles. Mainly we use the productive cycle to energize and the exhaustive cycle to remedy. Note that a seriously bad combination of numbers should be kept unused and not activated. Remedies may reduce ill effects but they cannot be completely overcome, especially when an incoming annual or monthly visiting star triggers their evil nature. So always watch annual and monthly stars.*
4 *Whether or not environmental features such as a straight oncoming road, a tall building, or heavy and fast-moving traffic act as triggers.*

Advanced Work on Flying Star

PART SIX

42. THE AUSPICIOUS SPECIALS

THERE ARE SEVERAL AUSPICIOUS SO-CALLED "SPECIALS" IN FLYING STAR WHICH PROMISE EXTREME GOOD FORTUNE WHEN THEY OCCUR IN THE FLYING STAR NATAL CHART, AND WHEN CERTAIN PHYSICAL MANIFESTATIONS ARE ALSO PRESENT. THESE TWO AND THREE NUMBER COMBINATIONS REFER TO COMBINATIONS OF THE PERIOD STAR NUMBER, THE WATER STAR NUMBER, AND/OR THE MOUNTAIN STAR NUMBER. NOT ALL THE NINE PERIODS HAVE THESE SPECIALS, SO IF YOU'RE PLANNING TO BUILD A HOME IT IS WORTH INVESTIGATING IF WAITING UNTIL THE CHANGE OF PERIOD WILL ALLOW YOU TO BENEFIT FROM ONE OF THESE COMBINATIONS.

When you become familiar with the numbers that constitute these specials you might be faced with the dilemma of not knowing which set of numbers to choose in building a new home. For example you may have to choose between tapping say a "double 8" or the "sum of ten." This is something that requires you to make a trade off. Or you may discover contradictions in the analysis – for instance the elements may be saying one thing and the numbers by themselves saying something else. In such instances take note of the strength of the specials. When they are very strong – i.e. when special combinations are supported by structures in the environment – they can and do override the elements. Think through how you wish to tap the numbers. Often solutions do come in a flash of brilliance and, with practice, you will grow in confidence. Be alert to results when making flying star changes. Believe me, feng shui results manifest very quickly. You will feel the change in energy within a week of making changes. So stay alert and live in a state of awareness – this is the best way to train yourself in the use of advanced feng shui.

We will look at each of the specials in turn.

1. The sum of ten

This is when two numbers in each palace combine to make the sum of 10 – an auspicious combination that suggests completeness and all five manifestations of happiness. The sum of ten brings an abundance of happiness, encompassing wealth, longevity, good health, a love of virtue, and excellent descendents luck. Significantly it also brings the promise of a natural death for residents so it protects against premature and violent death. The relevant combinations are of period star with water star or with mountain star and to qualify as sum of ten houses, all the palaces must have the sum of ten made up of two numbers. In the 180 years of a full cycle the sum of ten occurs 20 times in all the periods except in period five.

Period and water star sum of ten combinations are activated by the presence of water in the palace occupied by a prominent water star such as the water star 7 or the water star 8. Luck gets even better when the prominent water star is in the front of the house. And when there is also a mountain at the back palace, supporting the house, luck comes in abundance. Please note that when I say water I mean physical water or alternatively a hole, a valley, or lower ground. And when I say mountain I also include in my definition higher ground, a concrete wall, a building, or simply a mound of stones and rocks.

In looking at the strength of the sum of ten special some masters insist that they only work when the house is a perfect square or rectangle. A square house is said to be the most perfect manifestation but I have seen it work even in L-shaped houses.

A second condition of the sum of ten is that for it to have real strength it must be found in every single one of the nine palaces. Only then does it have the strength to override all other "rules" of the flying star system, including even the Five Yellow and other ominous indications. Such is the power of the sum of ten. There are sum of ten houses in all periods, except period five.

In period seven, for instance, you can see that a south 2/3 house is a real sum of ten house. In this illustration of the natal chart the sum of ten in every palace is highlighted. In addition I have also highlighted the prominent mountains stars 8 and 7, which should be activated to

Facing South 2 and 3

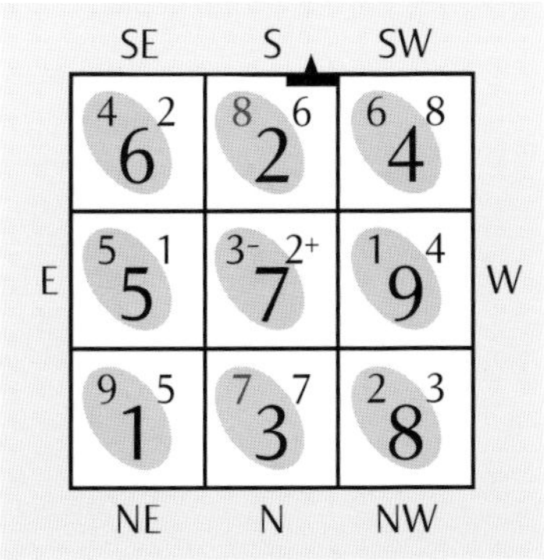

SE	S	SW
4 2 **6**	8 6 **2**	6 8 **4**
5 1 **5**	3- 2+ **7**	1 4 **9**
9 5 **1**	7 7 **3**	2 3 **8**

(E on left, W on right; NE, N, NW below)

get the most out of this sum of ten combination. To activate this particular combination (where the period star combines with the mountain star) use a crystal.

The third condition for the sum of ten is that for it to attain its full power it should be strongly activated by external land forms. Traditionally this meant having the celestial guardians – dragon and tiger, tortoise and phoenix – around the house. I have found, however, that the conditions can also be simulated with the use of good paintings of mountains as well as by using symbols of good fortune. For example, it is possible to use a quartz crystal "mountain" placed in the "small tai chi palace" or corner housing the prominent mountain star 8. This attracts power, recognition, influence, and patronage luck. Use a crystal that sends out strong vibes like a mountain.

Meanwhile, there are also charts where only certain sectors exhibit the sum of ten. In the following chart of a west 1-facing house the southeast palace has a period/mountain sum of ten, the southwest has a period/water sum of ten, and the east has a mountain/water sum of ten. This is not regarded as a sum of ten house, but the sum of ten in each of the palaces where they occur is still considered auspicious. This sum of ten, however, does not have the power to override other rules of flying star. However, the palaces can be individually activated – in the southeast and east with a water feature and in the southwest with a mountain feature to take advantage of the prominent star 7. Let the mountain star 3 fall into water to dissolve its quarrelsome instincts. Water features are best when they are Yang water.

Flying Star Feng Shui for the Master Practitioner

158

Facing West 1

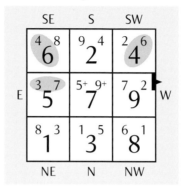

2. The parent string or three period combinations

This is a very powerful and very auspicious combination which manifests the luck of three periods. Wherever it occurs prosperity permeates through the household throughout the 20 years of that period. This combination is also referred to in the texts as the "parent string" of three numbers – with each number representing one of the lower, upper, and middle periods. The chart below shows how numbers are laid out in the three period table. The auspicious combinations are 1, 4, 7; 2, 5, 8; and 3, 6, 9.

These numbers represent truly awesome luck. When they are present in your flying star natal chart you and your family will enjoy tremendous good fortune in the form of wealth, fame, success, respect, recognition, family happiness, and harmony – as well as excellent descendants who bring honor to the family. Three periods simply means that the house will

Parent String Numbers

	Head	Body	Legs
Upper period	1	2	3
Middle period	4	5	6
Lower period	7	8	9

enjoy good fortune through the three periods. It suggests long-lasting good luck. And it also protects residents from premature and violent death. So these are wonderful combinations to have.

When building a new home you might want to design it around a natal chart that manifests these numbers. They occur in the coming period of eight in houses that tap the SW/NE axis in the second or third sub-directions as their facing orientation. So houses facing NE/SW 2/3 will enjoy the parent string formation. The relevant period eight charts are shown below.

Most texts recommend that the presence of these numbers should be cause enough for good fortune to manifest. There are some practitioners, however, who insist that the cosmic trinity of heaven, earth, and mankind represented by this combination requires the presence of mountains in front and slow-moving water behind for its good fortune to be released. This is something fairly controversial and I am personally reluctant to interpret the texts this way since mountains in front of the house seldom bring good luck and in fact it signifies that one's luck is blocked. Water behind also signifies missed opportunity.

I would interpret this special as being so auspicious it does not require the traditional mountain behind and water in front formation, and even when there is a mountain in front and slow moving water behind it continues to be auspicious. So as long as the parent string numbers are present in every palace of the natal chart this alone should signify extreme good fortune. This configuration of numbers does not occur in periods one, three, seven, and nine. It occurs in the earth periods of two, five, and eight, and it occurs twice in periods four and six.

Southwest 2/3-Facing Door

	S	SW	W	
	6 9 **3**	8 2 **5**	4 7 **1**	
SE	1 4 **7**	2 5 **8**	3 6 **9**	NW
	9 3 **6**	5 8 **2**	7 1 **4**	
	E	NE	N	

Northeast 2/3-Facing Door

	N	NE	E	
	1 7 **4**	8 5 **2**	3 9 **6**	
NW	6 3 **9**	5 2 **8**	4 1 **7**	SE
	7 4 **1**	2 8 **5**	9 6 **3**	
	W	SW	S	

So in the coming period of eight this auspicious combination is available to be tapped (more on this in the chapter on Changing to Period Eight).

3. The pearl string sequential combination

In addition to the parent string combination of three period numbers there is another "special" combination of numbers that is also auspicious. This is the three sequential number combination. For this special to have real strength, the combination has to be present in every palace of the house. An excellent example of the occurrence of these numbers can be seen in a NW2/3-facing house.

When they occur in a chart they have the power to triple any kind of good luck activated. Here is the chart of a period seven house with the facing orientation NW2/3. Look at how every sector in this chart shows a sequential range of numbers. Such a house would also benefit from having mountains in the distance in front of the home and water behind. The texts do, however, warn that all benefits expire and must be revitalized at the end of the period. In the case of this house that means on 4 February 2004 residents of such a house should immediately change the period of the house to period eight.

An important note regarding this feature touches on how it can be activated. To manifest extreme good fortune the presence of a range of mountains in the distance in front of the home is required. Such homes will enjoy tremendous good fortune, especially when it is

Northwest 2/3-Facing House

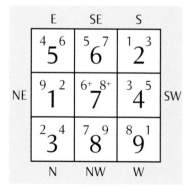

possible to see three discernible peaks. This feature indicates that the house will give birth to a child who will grow up to be emperor. Legend has it that the family home of the late Chinese leader Deng Xiao Ping was such a house. Those living in a house with such a chart should activate the prominent water and mountain stars with water and mountain features and symbols. The sequential bonus will triple the luck activated.

4. The structural strength of the auspicious doubles

The fourth of the auspicious specials manifests in the structural strength of auspicious doubles. These must not be missed or underestimated, especially when they occur in the facing palace in the front of the house or in the sitting palace at the back of the house. Either way when they occur as prominent numbers they bring an abundance of good fortune. These auspicious doubles occur in the charts of period seven and period eight, so remember to look out for the double 7 and the double 8.

Shown here are two charts with the auspicious doubles in the facing palace. This single indication alone can bring extreme good fortune, especially when properly energized. The period seven house is facing NE2/3 and the period eight house is facing north 1. In case you are trying to follow the path of the stars, just note that the period seven chart is in the original format with south placed on the top, while the period eight chart has already been turned to place north on top. This is sometimes done to make analysis easier, so don't get confused.

Period 7 House

	SE	S	SW	
	3 2 **6**	8 6 **2**	1 4 **4**	
E	2 3 **5**	4+ 1- **7**	6 8 **9**	W
	7 7 **1**	9 5 **3**	5 9 **8**	
	NE	N	NW	

Period 8 House

	NW	N	NE	
	4 3 **9**	8 8 **4**	6 1 **2**	
W	5 2 **1**	3 4 **8**	1 6 **6**	E
	9 7 **5**	7 9 **3**	2 5 **7**	
	SW	S	SE	

These exceptionally good indications should be energized. In the period seven house, where the double 7 occurs in the facing palace, the texts say that if there are real mountains in the distance that are within view, and there is also water nearby, then there will be outstanding overall luck. In charts where the double 7 is in the sitting palace then having both water and mountains behind the house would be most beneficial. When we speak of mountains here we are referring to the real physical presence of mountains. In cities tall buildings can take the place of mountains.

Where physical mountains and water are not available, man-made water and specially-built hillocks can fulfill the same function. The only condition is to ensure the water and mountain are within view but not too close to the home. They should not appear to block the home, so when mountains in front are required to activate the auspicious star it is best when they are at a distance. Charts with the double 8 in the period of eight will also bring great abundance when activated in a similar fashion.

43. THE UNIQUE SITUATIONS

In advanced flying star charts it is necessary to be on the look out for unique situations where either the configuration of numbers or their presence in any specific palace requires special attention. I have loosely categorized the more important of these as "unique situations."

I do recommend that you make a checklist of these situations, so that your practice of flying star becomes more complete. Most times these situations call for the presence of water or a mountain either at the back or front of the home. Remember that water can mean real water placed in a small container like an urn or a wide-mouthed vase or it can mean a hole in the ground. Water is always an excellent energizer and when there are unique situations that call for it to be present arrange something special such as an auspicious goldfish pond or water feature. The oxygenation activates the water while fish and plants bring in Sheng chi. Do not, however, make it too large as this will compromise balance.

Obviously mountains are not as easy to conjure up as the presence of water. However, we can create a symbolic representation of them. What I do is make my own mountains with the symbolic placement of stones, boulders, and even crystals. Ensure your boulders are big enough to represent mountains but not so large that they block the chi. To create my "mountain" I used three solid rocks which I placed near my front door. Each rock was supposed to represent each member of my direct family – my husband, my daughter, and myself. I obtained the rocks from the property of a very old rich family whose lineage I respect so they had excellent chi as well. This was to activate the auspicious mountain star in my facing palace as well as one of the unique situations described below.

When going through these unique situations take note of water and mountain requirements.

1. Palaces of the direct and indirect chi

One of the secret ways of analyzing the chi distribution of the natal chart is by identifying the palace of the direct chi and the palace of the indirect chi in any period. According to the ancient texts, the palace of the direct chi is where the period number is located in the original Lo Shu square.

Hence in the period of seven the palace of direct chi is the west palace. This is because the number 7 is placed in the west in the original Lo Shu square. And the palace of the indirect chi is directly opposite, so in the period of seven this will be the east. In the original Lo Shu square note that the direct and indirect chi always add up to 10. In all periods other than in period five, the indirect chi is always the place of the Five Yellow. Hence in period seven, the indirect chi is in the east palace. This is also where the 5 is located in a period seven chart.

In period eight the direct chi is in the northeast palace while the indirect chi is in the southwest. So during period eight the Five Yellow flies to the southwest palace.

To correctly enhance the palaces of the direct and indirect chi the texts advise that there should be water in the palace of the indirect chi, but there should never be water in the palace of the direct chi. At a practical level this is how you can harvest the direct and indirect chi:

* *Place a small water feature in the east palace in the period of seven, as this is the palace of the indirect chi. The water here will activate excellent good fortune as it churns up growth energy. In terms of the elements, water in the east is also good since this is a wood sector that benefits*

directly from the presence of water. In the cycle of elements water produces wood. Do not have symbols representing mountains in the east.

- *In the period of eight this same water feature should be moved to the southwest. This is an earth sector but having water in this particular part of the house is excellent. The water feature need not be too large. An excellent suggestion is to have a water lily or a lotus pond in a wide-brimmed pot. In my own home I use a special urn with the double dragon design (the presence of dragons near water is an added energizer) and I place this in the part of the garden that falls within the east palace. Of course, I intend to move this water feature to the southwest once period eight is upon us.*

- *Inside the house it is also a good idea to consider placing small water features in the corners of the living room and dining room that correspond to the east palace. This will energize the indirect chi of the room to bring in wealth and added income luck.*

- *Note, however, that it will be disastrous to have water in the west during the period of seven. This is because water in the palace of the direct chi clashes badly with the sector. Also note that in the cycle of the elements water exhausts metal. Hence it is vital to observe this cardinal taboo of the period of seven. So do not place water in the west palace in the period of seven and observe this same rule for the northeast in the period of eight. Instead of water there should be the presence of a mountain in the palace of the direct chi, so a wall or a tall part of the house in this sector of the building is exceptionally auspicious.*

2. Hidden misfortune stars in the heart palace – the 5

The texts also warn of situations when the deadly Five Yellow flies into the heart palace, i.e. into the center of the home, either as the water star or as the mountain star. This is a configuration that brings misfortunes to the household unless remedial measures are taken to contain its malevolent influence. This situation is described as having "hidden misfortune stars in the heart of the home."

The manifestation of the Five Yellow in the heart palace can be hidden or obvious in nature, depending on whether the 5 flies positive or negative. Both are troublesome and inconvenient but differ in severity of affliction. When the 5 flies positive in a plus mode its evil negative nature is hidden and is therefore more deadly, as it causes misfortune to strike without warning. Loss, illness, or accidents occur without warning. This is known as the hidden misfortune. When the 5 flies negative in a minus mode its nature is said to be more obvious.

In the period of seven the number 5 will fly into the center as the water star when the house is facing east. When the facing direction is east 1 it will fly positive and when the facing direction is east 2/3 it will fly negative. The number 5 flies to the center as the mountain star when the house is facing west. It flies positive when the house is facing west 1 and it flies negative when the house is facing west 2/3.

There are effective remedies to control these "misfortune" stars. The first is to place a "mountain of gold" in the center of the home. This can be in the form of a painting, real crystals, or a rockery design. The second method is simply to keep a pile of Chinese coins in the center of the home. A third possibility is the use of metallic windchimes (six rods), and the final and most novel way of keeping this troublesome 5 under control is by imprisoning it in a small cell in the center of the home. This causes the Five Yellow to lose its ability to cause mischief. Obviously if you already have a small toilet or storeroom in the center of your house or apartment this will do very nicely. It serves as a convenient cell for the misfortune star.

Please note that if, for whatever reason, you inadvertently change the facing direction of your home (eg. by using another entrance door as the main door or when renovating the house) and that causes an auspicious prominent star like 7 or 8 to fly into the heart of the home then you must make certain that this auspicious star is not trapped in any small toilet or storeroom there. When the auspicious water star gets trapped in this way it will lead to severe financial loss for the residents; when the auspicious mountain star gets trapped this way it will lead to health problems that could develop into something fatal. The solution is either to use another door thereby changing the whole natal chart or tear down the cell that imprisons the auspicious stars.

Do, however, take comfort from the fact that when the facing or sitting palace of the house contains other auspicious and prominent stars, they can develop sufficient chi to override the misfortunes created in the heart palace.

3. Remedying a situation of excessive Yin – the 4/9/2/7

This is a situation that can lead to rooms becoming haunted and, more significantly, women not being able to find husbands or losing their husbands to predatory females. Excessive Yin unleashes the negative side of the female energy. The focus in flying star is not just on the numbers of the natal chart and their attributes but also on the Yin and Yang of the numbers and the palaces they fly into. Numbers as well as palaces are categorized as being Yin or Yang.

Basically the Yin numbers of flying star are 9, 4, 2, and 7, and the Yin palaces are the south, the southeast, the southwest, and the west. These are also described as the "female rooms" of the home. If you look at the illustration below it is easy to visualize where these Yin sectors are. Generally speaking, rooms located in the Yin palaces should not have a surplus of Yin numbers otherwise there develops a situation of excessive Yin chi. When such rooms are also kept dark, or painted in somber Yin colors, the room tends to attract wandering spirits. I have never been to a haunted house but I have been told of too many creepy experiences to want to take the risk of having this excessive Yin affliction.

What is probably of greater interest is that when there is excessive Yin chi, the male energy can become seriously depleted. So even when such households do not have to endure haunting, the men who live in such homes tend to fall easy prey to predatory females. Homes afflicted with excessive Yin energy tend to have more than their fair share of problems relating to love, romance, and marriage (or lack of it). Young men of such households also tend to get trapped in unfortunate situations with undesirable women, especially women who bring bad luck to them. Such women are described as "women with broomstick destiny" – they sweep away all the good luck in their men's lives. So excessive Yin is definitely a serious affliction.

Yin & Yang of Flying Star Numbers

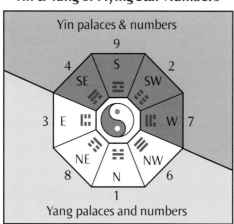

Women living in such homes will also find it difficult to get married, or to meet eligible members of the opposite sex. This becomes severe when the Yin sectors get overgrown with large leafy trees that completely block out the sunlight. In such homes Yin in excess creates a total collapse of marriage luck for the women of the household.

The house illustrated on the following page has the potential to develop this Yin chi dominated affliction. This is a period seven house that has a west 1-facing direction. In this house notice that the south palace and the west palace are both Yin palaces but they also both have a collection of Yin numbers. The south palace has the Yin numbers 9, 2, 4 and the west palace has the Yin numbers 7, 9, 2. Now note that the master bedroom is located in the south palace.

The main door is located in the west palace, which is also the facing palace. Now look at the thick growth of trees surrounding the Yin side of the house. These trees cause sunlight to get blocked. If the bedroom is also painted in Yin-dominated colors (dark colors) and if it is poorly lit with thick drape curtains the room will become Yin dominated very easily, transforming it into a seriously afflicted palace. What needs to be done to introduce more Yang energy?

- *The room would benefit from being painted white.*
- *Bright lights should be installed.*
- *The trees outside should be trimmed.*
- *Brighter colored curtains would do wonders.*
- *A single red lamp could be introduced to strongly counter the excessive Yin.*

As for the facing palace, where the main door is located, this too should be brightly lit. In fact keeping the whole house bright with good and clever lighting, hanging Yang colors and paintings, and bringing in the sunshine by hanging faceted crystals along the open bay windows is the best way of overcoming the excessive Yin situation here.

Period 7 House Facing West 1

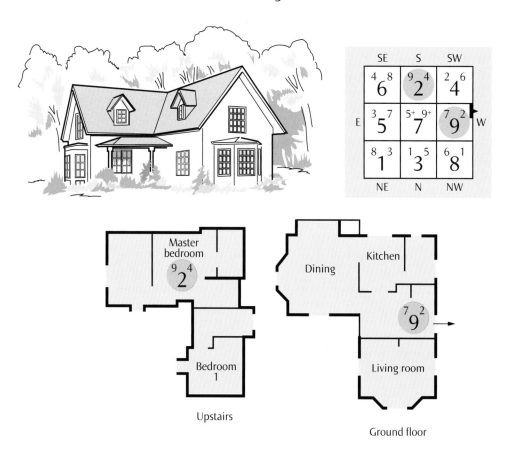

Upstairs

Ground floor

4. Fire at heaven's gate – the 6/9

This is a very well known affliction that is also observed under other systems of feng shui. Basically it refers to having open fire energy in the northwest, which stands for heaven. The northwest is the place of the trigram Chien so this is a very important sector in any house. Chien controls the luck of the head of the household. It also governs the house's patronage luck. Its element is big metal, an element that gets destroyed by fire energy. Thus feng shui masters generally advice their clients never to locate the kitchen in the northwest of the house. If the kitchen is placed here the remedy is to use water and earth energy – water to overcome the fire and earth to strengthen the metal. However, if you can avoid having the kitchen here do so.

Definitely avoid having the stove in the northwest. I would also go so far as to place a caveat on fireplaces. These too should not be in the northwest of the house or of the rooms where they are found.

In flying star "fire at heaven's gate" is indicated by the combination of 6 and 9. Wherever this combination is found, even when it is not in the northwest palace, it is disastrous to have the kitchen, stove, or fireplace there. Moreover, anything sharp, red, or excessively bright also activates the numbers. Sharp pointed buildings in the near horizon also cause these stars to get activated. What is the result of this affliction?

- *It causes illness to residents of the palace where it occurs.*
- *More specifically, it can cause the development of lung cancer so those staying in such rooms must not smoke as this activates the stars in the most dangerous way. In the old texts, the affliction of fire at heaven's gate is described as people vomiting blood. So the danger is very real.*
- *When the father stays in a room with this affliction he will lose his livelihood.*
- *When food is cooked in this sector the authority of the father will be challenged at home (by his children) and at work (by his employees). There will be plenty of problems!*
- *Finally, in the most negative manifestation, actual fire could cause the house to be burnt to the ground.*

In the period of seven the 6/9 combination does not occur in combinations of the mountain and water star. The affliction of fire at heaven's gate is thus manifested when the 9 star flies into the northwest palace as a mountain star. This happens in a SE2-facing house, so here it is advisable to ensure that no fireplaces, stoves, or sharp pointed objects are placed in the northwest palace.

In the period of eight there are 6/9 combinations found in houses that have facing directions along the SW/NE axis. However, these houses also have the parent string combinations, and these have the power to override the 6/9. Still it is advisable to treat the 6/9 combination with respect.

5. Hostile wind brings illness and in-law problems – the 4/2

One of the more serious indications in flying star combinations is the 4 and 2 combination. Occurring as water and mountains star combinations these two numbers manifest the wind of the number 4 and the earth and illness indication of the number 2. Wind over earth suggests wind scattering the dust everywhere, a situation that requires observation and patience. The two numbers also suggest two women clashing – the wife and the older woman (mother-in-law). So there could be problems for the wife or the mother who occupies a room with this combination.

And since 2 is the illness star, this combination also indicates the wind of 4 causing illness to manifest. It is possible to get an idea of what kind of illness is indicated by looking at the sector which has this 2/4 combination – although the number 2 almost always suggests problems of the abdomen, stomach, and womb. The presence of the 4/2 combination in each sector can suggest specific problems:

- *In the wood sectors southeast and east it indicates health problems related to the liver and bladder. It can also suggest accidents related to the limbs – legs, hands, fingers, toes.*
- *In the water sector north it indicates health problems related to the kidneys and the ears.*
- *In the metal sectors west and northwest it indicates problems with the bones and the lungs.*
- *In the earth sectors southwest, the center of the house, or northeast it indicates health problems related to the abdomen, the head, and also mental afflictions.*
- *In the fire sector south it indicates health problems related to the heart and the eyes.*

At a practical level, the health problems associated with the 2/4 combination seem to manifest most often in situations where there is a bed in the sector afflicted by it. This is shown in the period 7 house illustrated here. This NW2-facing house has the 2/4 combination in the north palace. This room is occupied by the grandmother of the house and her bed is situated in the place of the 2/4 combination, therefore exposing her to its ill-effects. If it is not possible to move to another room, then the concept of small tai chi can be applied to the bedroom. This involves superimposing the whole chart onto only the bedroom. By doing this you will discover exactly where not to place the bed to avoid the worst effects of the combination.

Period 7 House Facing NW2

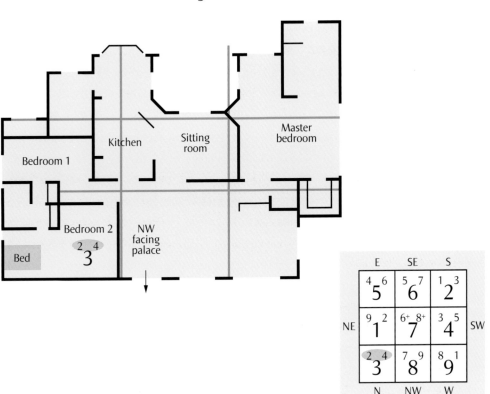

Kitchen

Sitting room

Master bedroom

Bedroom 1

Bedroom 2

NW facing palace

$2\ 4$
3

Bed

	E	SE	S	
	${}^4\,{}^6$ 5	${}^5\,{}^7$ 6	${}^1\,{}^3$ 2	
NE	${}^9\,{}^2$ 1	${}^{6^+}\,{}^{8^+}$ 7	${}^3\,{}^5$ 4	SW
	${}^2\,{}^4$ 3	${}^7\,{}^9$ 8	${}^8\,{}^1$ 9	
	N	NW	W	

6. Literary and academic success with the 4/1

I guess mine is the best example of how to benefit from the literary combination of 4 and 1 and to a lesser extent the 1 and 4 where the stars involved are the mountain and water stars. My home is a period seven house facing the SW1 direction. So I have the wonderful 4/1 combination in my sitting palace where the mountain star is 4 and the water star is 1. This is an excellent situation and since it was the mountain (sitting) star I needed to activate, it was fortuitous that I had a natural "mountain" at the back of the house. This took the form of elevated land that has an armchair appearance. I did not need to activate the combination further. The 4/1 combination brought me a great deal of literary luck – my books have done well and I have succeeded in carving out a good career as a writer. In addition, my heart palace also has the combination of 1, 4, and 7. As you will recall, this is a parent string combination which makes it intrinsically a good combination – but the significance of this combination is the 4 water star and the 1 mountain star in the center.

In the apartment below, the facing palace has the 1/4 while the heart palace has the 4/1 – a combination that will benefit resident's academic and literary luck. Note also that the master bedroom benefits from the double 7, the second bedroom benefits from the mountain star 8, and the kitchen presses down on the 9/5.

The 4/1 and 1 and 4 combination occurs in many of the period seven charts and it is useful to take note of subtle differences in the luck created, depending on whether it is the mountain or water star that has the 4 and the 1. Many of the old texts suggest that the 4/1 combination indicates luck associated with scholarly and academic pursuits – careers that have to do with writing and research. As long as these two numbers occur together in the same palace this is what they have the potential to bring. But the two numbers also have another more interesting dimension and this is the indication of romantic entanglements, mainly involving the male residents fooling around with women outside the family. This latter reading is said to be activated by the presence of water. Thus here is a case where the productive elements of 1 and 4 (water producing wood) are already sufficient in and of themselves. The texts warn against the danger of sexual scandals

Apartment with NE1-Facing Chart

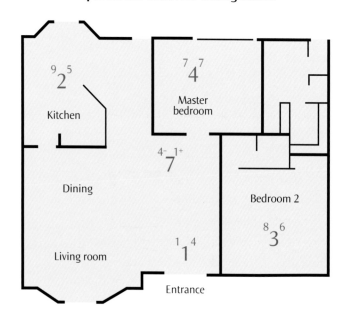

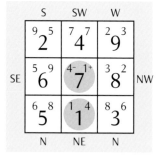

that could arise if the 4/1 or 1 and 4 are activated by excess water. To be on the safe side, it is better to let your college-going children tap into the good effects of this combination by placing them in bedrooms with this combination. Leave water out of it altogether, otherwise you run the risk of unleashing the seductive siren that lies hidden in the 1 and 4 combination.

7. The fighting stars – the 3/2

One of the more common afflictions in period seven charts is the occurrence of the horrible 2 and 3 combination which is colorfully described as quarrelling chi that is so fierce it is like two bulls fighting! Here both numbers are negative numbers and show their ugly side in the period of seven. The number 2 suggests mental tensions and worries while the number 3 denotes disputes, legal problems, calamities, and litigation. Together the two numbers also reflect the destructive result of wood hurting earth. Businesses afflicted by this combination will face very severe problems, while homes with this combination in their charts will experience fights between residents, as well as with people from outside the family. The affliction becomes truly severe when this combination occurs in either the facing or sitting palace.

Period 7 House Facing North 2

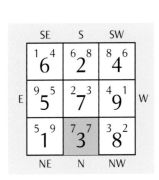

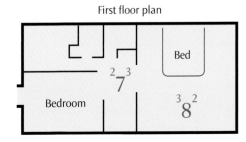

First floor plan

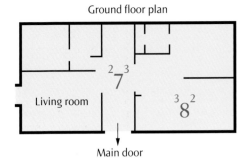

Ground floor plan

Married couples who move into a home afflicted with the 3/2 have a hard time staying together. Divorces and separations will be the result. The best way to deal with this serious problem is to avoid it altogether, i.e. move out of a room afflicted with the 3/2 and try to relocate a main door that is afflicted into a more auspicious palace. In the small tai chi application of this affliction, even the bed position should not be where the 3/2 resides within the bedroom. Note that in the previous illustration, the 3/2 is in the master bedroom but the bed itself successfully taps the auspicious stars of the southwest. In placing the bed here, the effect of the 3/2 is reduced.

If it is not possible to move out of an afflicted room, or to move an afflicted door, the suggested remedy is to use what I call Yin fire energy to exhaust the 3 and Yin metal to tire out the 2. This means introducing red-and-gold-colored decorations that have no life. These colors suggest the elements but are still and very Yin. When there is no life in the elements they can exhaust the 3/2 without causing it to become activated. Yin fire cannot feed the earth 2 but it can exhaust the jade 3. So if your bedroom is afflicted you might want to consider using gold/red curtains to suppress. A small red light is also effective as long as it is not too overwhelming. And suitable art will also be very effective. Note that the placement of twinkling lights, crystal chandeliers, moving windchimes, mobiles, television sets, computers, clocks, or anything that suggests movement will activate the 3/2. So avoid such items.

8. The misfortune combinations – the 5/2 and 5/9

Spotting and disarming the influence of the combinations that comprise the deadly five – the 5 with the 2 and the 5 with the 9 – is really not part of advanced feng shui because these combinations are so bad they are among the first star combinations to look out for. Every amateur Flying Star feng shui enthusiast should be alert to the dangers that a 2/5 or 5/2 combination brings. They cause misfortunes, loss, and bad luck, irrespective of how they combine. There are no subtleties about the 5 and the 2 – they are simply bad news in this period and in the next so I hope this has come across by now. Be on your guard.

The 2 and 5 combination becomes part of advanced feng shui analysis when it cannot be overcome with simple cures. When you really cannot cope with the 5 and 2 and they really are bringing all the manifestations of bad luck – accidents, major illnesses, serious financial problems, and other tragedies – there are additional things that can be done to control them.

Under normal circumstances metal windchimes comprising six rods are adequate to control the 5/2. The stronger they are, for example when their energy is helped along by visiting annual and month 5/2 stars, the greater the number of windchimes required. However, when this cure is insufficient what you can do is obtain six large metal coins (those with a square hole in the center), tie these together in a row and position them high up on the wall. If the affliction is at the facing palace, place these six coins in a row above the door. Then place another six coins in a row on the floor and cover it with a rug or carpet. The Yin metal energy of the coins will keep the 5/2 under control.

A second method is to create a small room in the palace where the 5/2 occurs and imprison the numbers inside. Make sure the door into the room is kept locked. This is a method that has been known to work quite effectively. The only problem is that the suppressed negative energy needs an outlet so it is necessary to air the room regularly. This causes the bad chi to dissipate.

In this period seven house the 5/9 and 9/5 are in the west and southwest, directly affecting the luck of the master bedroom. This room needs a blue carpet and a large brass urn to keep the 5/9 under control. The 9/5 in the bathroom can be said to be pressed down by the toilet.

As far as 5/9 and 9/5 combinations are concerned, note that under certain circumstances these can cause even more severe bad luck. While the 2 brings illness to add to the travails of

Period 7 House Facing North 1

SE	S	SW
3 2 **6**	7 7 **2**	5 9 **4**
4 1 **5**	2 3 **7**	9 5 **9**
8 6 **1**	6 8 **3**	1 4 **8**
NE	N	NW

(E at left, W at right)

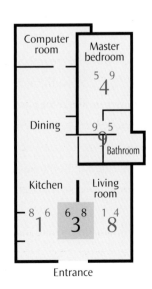

Entrance

the 5, the 9 strengthens the 5. This is because 9 is fire and fire produces earth. Nine is also a magnifying star. It makes good star numbers luckier and makes unlucky star numbers truly deadly! To control the 9/5 use a brass urn filled with still water (don't use this cure in the bedroom). The metal controls the 5 while the water puts out the fire. In the bedroom the use of water is never a good thing so it is necessary to use the color blue instead. Do still use metal, however, as the use of metal to exhaust the 5 is more vital than water.

44. THE HO TU NUMBER COMBINATIONS

The Ho Tu combination of numbers can herald very good fortune or they can warn against specific dangers when they appear in certain palaces. Usually Ho Tu numbers are used extensively in the analysis of feng shui for Yin dwellings – however they also have meaning in Yang dwelling charts. An interesting aside on Ho Tu numbers is that they also indicate excellent compatibility between two people. Thus two people having Kua numbers that make up any one of the four Ho Tu combinations are said to be very good for each other.

There are four Ho Tu combinations of numbers:

1 and 6 The element of this combination is water and their original direction is north, but they indicate auspicious earth chi, which brings excellent happiness luck. Social life, marriage, and romance benefit from good healthy chi for residents affected by this combination. Where it is found, activate with earth energy symbolized by stones, boulders, rocks, and crystal. When there are mountains in the direction of the Ho Tu 6/1, it gets activated. An example of a 6/1 combination is found in the southeast palace of a period seven house that faces west 2/3 (see chart).

2 and 7 The element of these two numbers is fire and their original direction is south, but they indicate gold chi – which suggests growth in family wealth, landed property, and other assets. When this number occurs in the natal charts it is absolutely brilliant to activate with fake gold ingots and other gold-looking indications of wealth such as coins and auspicious symbols made in gold.

Period 7 House Facing West 2/3

SE	S	SW
6 1 **6**	1 5 **2**	8 3 **4**
7 2 **5**	5- 9- **7**	3 7 **9**
2 6 **1**	9 4 **3**	4 8 **8**
NE	N	NW

E ... W

Period 7 House Facing East 1

SE	S	SW
8 4 **6**	4 9 **2**	6 2 **4**
7 3 **5**	9+ 5+ **7**	2 7 **9**
3 8 **1**	5 1 **3**	1 6 **8**
NE	N	NW

E ... W

3 and 8 The element of these two numbers is wood and their original direction is east, but they indicate water chi, which also means prosperity, and money and cash flowing into the family. It can also refer to the luck of career and the luck associated with employment. When energized by water these numbers bring good fortune very quickly. An example of the 3/8 combination in the period of seven can be found in an east 1-facing house (see chart).

4 and 9 The element of these two numbers is metal and their original direction is west, but they indicate growth chi which is one of the best types of luck to have. It suggests expansion, getting bigger, amassing wealth, and gaining in influence and power. Sheng chi is often interpreted as being better than mere money luck. When present in the facing palace it is most auspicious. However, the 4/9 combination must be correctly activated with a pointed fire mountain in the front of the house some distance away. The 4/9 is also present in an east 1-facing house of the period seven.

These Ho Tu combinations must comprise the mountain and water stars. Combinations involving the period star do not count in the above interpretations.

The Ho Tu cycles create another set of criteria

There is another set of conditions that involve a combination of the period and the water star
or mountain star, or the water and mountain star. Here there are specific meanings attached
to Ho Tu numbers depending on whether the cycle is waxing, thereby bringing good fortune;
or destructive, thereby bringing misfortune. When the cycle is destructive, or waning, the Ho
Tu numbers bring severe tragedy. It is therefore important to guard against this. Note that this
criteria on combinations takes effect only when they are present in the palace where the main
door of the house is located. When they occur anywhere else, the Ho Tu numbers hold no
meanings. They only count when present in the facing palace.

When the Cycle is waxing:

1 and 6 bring excellent education luck.
The house will produce lots of intelligent and talented children.
1 and 6 is in the waxing cycle in the east and southeast.
It is at its height in the north.

2 and 7 bring financial bonanzas.
Unfortunately the money could be tainted, so the luck is mixed.
2 and 7 is in the waxing cycle in the southwest and northeast.
It is at its height in the south.

3 and 8 bring success in politics.
There is also descendants' luck but children tend to be independent minded.
3 and 8 are in the waxing cycle in the south palace.
It is at its height in the east and southeast palaces.

4 and 9 bring business luck.
Money is made through ethical means.
4 and 9 is in the waxing cycle in the north.
It is at its height on the west and northwest palaces.

When the Cycle is destructive:

1 and 6 brings accidents to the patriarch.
Descendants bring shame to the family. Very sad and tragic.
1 and 6 is in the destructive cycle in the south so beware.

2 and 7 leads to infant deaths.
Illness and accidents can be fatal.
2 and 7 is destructive in the northwest and west. Be careful of these sectors.

3 and 8 leads to death by suicide.
Children may die prematurely.
3 and 8 is destructive when it appears in the southwest palace.

4 and 9 leads to injury and death in war.
Children could become orphans.
4 and 9 is destructive in the east palace.

45. FLIGHT OF WATER AND MOUNTAIN STARS

In the construction of the flying star natal chart there are four flight patterns of the mountain and water stars and these reflect either a Yin or a Yang aspect. It is Yin when the numbers move in a minus or descending pattern. It is Yang when the numbers move in a plus or ascending pattern. The plus or minus flight pattern has implications on the luck of the house, depending on how they may be activated by the presence of mountains and water features. These can be natural or man made, although many senior practitioners in Hong Kong insist that natural formations always have more strength. They do admit, however, that in a city environment the effect of multi-level buildings, multi-level roads and man-made water features also have much strength and some are not any less powerful in creating a good or bad impact on the surrounding feng shui.

There are the four combinations of the flight of mountain and water stars. These are:

1 *Mountain flies plus and water flies minus. This is called the descending mountain condition.*
  This is very auspicious if the house has water in front of it.

2 *Mountain flies minus and water flies plus. This is called the ascending mountain condition. This is very auspicious if there is a mountain behind.*

3 *Mountain flies plus and water also flies plus. This is called the ascending mountain, descending water condition. This is very auspicious if there is mountain behind and water in front.*

4 *Mountain flies minus and water flies minus as well. This is called the reverse mountain and reverse water condition. This is very auspicious regardless of its position relative to water and mountain.*

46. EIGHT MANSIONS AND NINE PALACES

We have already seen that under Eight Mansions feng shui the formula describes eight types of chi energy in any home based on the facing direction of the house or building. This distribution of chi energy, which can be laid out in a chart, is not the same as the flying star chart which also describes the distribution and quality of chi in any house. However, while the Flying Star method describes nine palaces, the Eight Mansions formula describes eight mansions where the center grid is "ignored." Under flying star, the center grid is the all-important heart palace.

There are eight charts that lay out the Eight Mansions chi distribution of any house. This chi distribution is in accordance with the facing direction of the house, and here "directions" refer to the 45 degree angle of each of the eight cardinal and secondary directions (shown opposite). The eight types of chi are described as follows, four being auspicious and four being inauspicious.

Sheng chi is auspicious growth chi indicating prosperity, success, and growth. In Eight Mansions this is the best chi quality to have and is assumed to always be at the front door.

Tien Yi chi is the auspicious good health chi indicating robust good health, good stamina, and a happy healthy lifestyle and attitude.

Nien Yen chi is the auspicious family and romance chi which indicates happiness luck for the family, for marriage, and for all relationships. This is a potent chi to tap when one wants love or to improve the quality of a marriage.

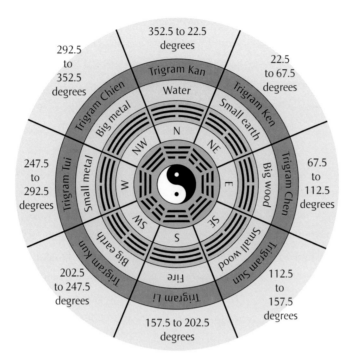

Fu Wei chi is the auspicious self-development chi. This brings great good luck to those engaged in pursuing knowledge and wisdom and hoping to grow. Tapping the Fu Wei chi of the home is excellent for those still engaged in academic study.

Ho Hai chi is the inauspicious chi that brings bad luck, disappointments, and setbacks.

Five Ghosts chi is the inauspicious chi that brings harmful people into one's life. This describes the luck of betrayal, of being cheated, and generally having "devil men" in one's life i.e. troublemakers and those who plot against you.

Six Killings chi is the inauspicious chi that brings the six types of bad luck. Nothing goes right. There are obstacles to success, blockages to wealth, accidents, loss, and illness. This chi is bad news and should be avoided.

Chueh Ming chi is the inauspicious total loss chi that brings the manifestations of bad luck. This can be very dangerous chi and can be extremely harmful when other indications also suggest bad chi, so it is a good idea to be wary.

The charts of houses with the eight types of chi laid out are derived from the facing direction of the house. Please note that the distribution of chi demarcates good and bad luck in the different "mansions" of the house and the house is either bad, good, or best for each of the different residents depending on their personal Kua numbers. It is their Kua numbers that indicate their personalized auspicious and inauspicious directions. In terms of auspicious and inauspicious locations, the house chi exerts greater influence than their personal auspicious locations, especially when it relates to which room they sleep and work in.

However, the Kua number can always be used to tap into personalized auspicious directions. So note the difference between direction and location. This is another way of saying "facing" and "sitting." The best situation is when the distribution of chi according to Eight Mansions also reflects your personalized best directions. This happens when the house is a west-group house and you are a west-group person or when the house is an east-group house and you are an east-group person. Opposite are the charts that spell out the chi distribution based on Eight Mansions. Take particular note of the north/south axis as well as the SW/NE axis houses as these are the houses that are specifically east or west group.

The first two charts belong to the north/south axis direction, meaning the house faces either north or south. These houses are east-group houses that bring beneficial luck to east-group people i.e. those with Kua numbers 1, 3, 4, and 9. Both the facing and sitting directions of this house belong to the east group. Examine the charts carefully and note that the Sheng chi direction is always in the part of the house where the front of the house is. Note also the chi (whether good or bad) of other sectors of the house.

The second two charts belong to the northeast/southwest axis direction, meaning the house faces either northeast or southwest. These houses are west-group houses that bring beneficial luck to west-group people i.e. those with Kua numbers 2, 5, 6, 7, and 8. Both the facing and sitting directions of this house belong to the west group. Examine the charts carefully and note once again the quality of the chi (whether beneficial or otherwise) in the other mansions.

In the four charts shown on page 184 note that these are *not* axis houses in that their facing and sitting directions belong to different groups – one is east and the other is west. These houses signify compromise situations where manifest chi is uncertain. This does not mean they are "bad" houses. It only means that both east- and west-group people can stay in such

Houses Facing the North/South Axis

a north-facing house

	SE	S	SW	
E	FU WEI personal growth	TIEN YI health	FIVE ghosts	**W**
	NIEN YEN romance	HOUSE sits SOUTH	SIX killings	
	CHUEH MING total loss	SHENG CHI success	HO HAI bad luck	
	NE	N	NW	

a south-facing house

	SE	S	SW	
E	NIEN YEN romance	SHENG CHI success	HO HAI bad luck	**W**
	FU WEI personal growth	HOUSE sits NORTH	CHUEH MING total loss	
	SIX killings	TIEN YI health	FIVE ghosts	
	NE	N	NW	

East-group houses excellent for east-group people

Houses Facing the NE/SW Axis

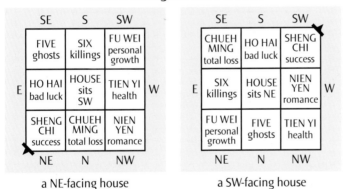

a NE-facing house

	SE	S	SW	
E	FIVE ghosts	SIX killings	FU WEI personal growth	**W**
	HO HAI bad luck	HOUSE sits SW	TIEN YI health	
	SHENG CHI success	CHUEH MING total loss	NIEN YEN romance	
	NE	N	NW	

a SW-facing house

	SE	S	SW	
E	CHUEH MING total loss	HO HAI bad luck	SHENG CHI success	**W**
	SIX killings	HOUSE sits NE	NIEN YEN romance	
	FU WEI personal growth	FIVE ghosts	TIEN YI health	
	NE	N	NW	

West-group houses excellent for west-group people

houses without having spectacularly good or bad luck. What is important is to examine the distribution of chi in the house and go on from there.

The Eight Mansions charts are excellent indicators of luck for the different parts of the house. Identify the chart that applies to your house and then check where your bedroom is located. Check whether you are tapping into the best chi distribution of the house.

**West Group House
a SE-Facing House**

SE	S	SW
SHENG CHI success	NIEN YEN romance	CHUEH MING total loss
TIEN YI health	HOUSE sits NW	HO HAI bad luck
FIVE ghosts	FU WEI personal growth	SIX killings

E (left) / W (right)

| NE | N | NW |

**East Group House
a NW-Facing House**

SE	S	SW
SIX killings	FIVE ghosts	TIEN YI health
CHUEH MING total loss	HOUSE sits SE	FU WEI personal growth
NIEN YEN romance	HO HAI bad luck	SHENG CHI success

E (left) / W (right)

| NE | N | NW |

These houses have different group facing and sitting directions

**West Group House
an E-Facing House**

SE	S	SW
TIEN YI health	FU WEI personal growth	SIX killings
SHENG CHI success	HOUSE sits WEST	FIVE ghosts
HO HAI bad luck	NIEN YEN romance	CHUEH MING total loss

E (left) / W (right)

| NE | N | NW |

**East Group House
a W-Facing House**

SE	S	SW
HO HAI bad luck	CHUEH MING total loss	NIEN YEN romance
FIVE ghosts	HOUSE sits EAST	SHENG CHI success
TIEN YI health	SIX killings	FU WEI personal growth

E (left) / W (right)

| NE | N | NW |

These houses have different group facing and sitting directions

The nine palaces

Once you have become familiar with your Eight Mansions charts, you can go deeper in your analysis of the luck of your house by narrowing down your reading of the facing direction to the 15 degree angles represented by the 24 mountains. So if your house happens to face north you now need to discover if it is facing north 1, north 2, or north 3. This applies to all eight directions so you have now a total of 24 directions. These are the 24 mountains, from which it is possible to derive the flying star natal chart. This exercise offers fresh new insights into the luck of the house. This next step basically combines the two charts derived from two different

24 Mountains of the Compass

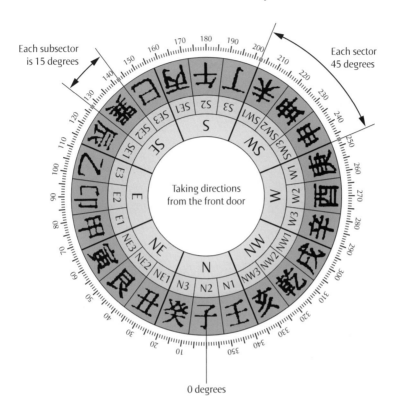

and separate formulas. The two formulas are not necessarily contradictory. The key to successful implementation of these two formulas is to know which "rule" overrides when it comes to a trade-off situation. More interesting is to understand how the energy changes depending on which of the three sub-sectors of directions the house faces. So here we are combining the eight mansions with the nine palaces.

The nine palaces of the natal chart indicate another dimension of chi. Please note that when powerfully prominent natal chart numbers are found in any sector, they transform inauspicious chi under eight mansions into overall auspicious chi.

On page 187 is an illustrated example of a SW1-facing house. The two charts on the right identify three very auspicious sectors in the house:

1   *The north palace, where the master bedroom is located. Under the eight mansions chart this sector has the Five Ghosts but under flying star it has the auspicious prominent 8 water star. This indicates a situation known as "five ghosts bringing gold" and is described in the texts as being particularly auspicious. When activated by water in the grounds of the north this house enjoys beneficial wealth luck.*

2   *The east palace, where the garage is located. Here the eight mansions chart indicates the Six Killings but the natal chart has the prominent mountain star 8 which thus "transforms the 6 killings into 6 nourishments." Once again bad luck transforms into unexpected very good luck.*

3   *The southwest palace, where the double seven is located. Here prominent stars for the period of seven combine with the growth energy of the eight mansions formula to bring exceptional and abundant good luck. With the door located here, and if there are no afflictions caused by poison arrows in the environment, residents of this house enjoy a smooth, happy life.*

If the house were facing SW2 or SW3 the flying star natal chart changes so that north becomes a dangerous sector. This is because the 5/9 combination of the natal chart reacts negatively with the Five Ghosts sector causing the north to be the sector where losses could occur. With the master bedroom located here this configuration of the charts does not augur well for the master and mistress of the house. You can check out the numbers in each of the palaces by checking the SW2 natal chart illustrated here. Note the numbers in the north are 5, 3, and 9 and this strengthens the evil influence of the Five Ghosts in the master bedroom. Meanwhile, note the numbers in the east sector, which has the Six Killings. Here energy is made worse by the horrible killing energy of 3/2. The numbers in the east are 3, 5, and 2. From this example you can see that if you wish you can take the analysis of flying stars further by combining the luck of nine palaces with the chi distribution of the eight mansions.

47. SPECIAL NOTES ON PLACEMENT OF WATER

There are special guidelines on the placement of water. The first guideline is that during periods of one, two, three, and four the water feature should be in the sectors of 6, 7, 8, or 9. In the periods of six, seven, eight, and nine, however, water features should be in the sectors 1, 2, 3, or 4. During the period of five, the water for the first 10 years should be in the sectors 1, 2, 3, or 4 and for the second 10 years should be in the sectors 6, 7, 8, or 9.

SW1-Facing Single Storey House

Master bedroom
5 GHOSTS BRING GOLD

Garage

SIX KILLINGS TRANSFORMED

Inside courtyard

Bedroom 1

Family foyer

Bedroom 2

SHENG CHI success | 7 7 / 4 | Dining

Entrance

Flying star

	N	NE	E	
	6 8 / 3	4 1 / 1	8 6 / 5	
NW	2 3 / 8	1+ 4- / 7	9 5 / 6	SE
	3 2 / 9	7 7 / 4	5 9 / 2	
	W	SW	S	

Eight mansions

	N	NE	E	
	FIVE ghosts	FU WEI personal growth	SIX killings	
NW	TIEN YI health	HOUSE sits KEN	CHUEH MING total loss	SE
	NIEN YEN romance	SHENG CHI success	HO HAI bad luck	
	W	SW	S	

	SE	S	SW	
	2 3 / 6	6 8 / 2	4 1 / 4	
E	3 2 / 5	1- 4+ / 7	8 6 / 9	W
	7 7 / 1	5 9 / 3	9 5 / 8	
	NE	N	NW	

Natal chart of a house facing SW2

Based on this guideline, water in this period of seven must be placed in sectors 1, 2, 3, or 4 if it is to be auspicious. To find out what these sectors are, simply refer to the original Lo Shu square, the one with the 5 in the center. This will tell you that sector 1 refers to the north, sector 2 to the southwest, sector 3 to the east, and sector 4 to the southeast. So as a general rule water features bring beneficial chi when placed in these sectors of your house.

This means that during this period up to the year 2004, any water feature built in the garden and located in one of these four directions will bring good fortune. Now please note that these continue to be the same four sectors that benefit from water for the next 20-year period i.e. during the period of eight. So whatever water feature you build now can continue to auspicious up to 4 February 2024.

But exactly which sector is the most auspicious for water ?

To attract seriously good feng shui you need to pinpoint which of these four sectors is the most auspicious spot. A quick formula pinpoints east as a very auspicious spot to place the water feature. This is because the Lo Shu number of the east in the original square is 3, and when 3 gets added to the number of this period – i.e. 3+7 – it equals 10, making it auspicious! Using this same method you will see that in the next period of eight, the lucky location will be 2 i.e. the southwest. This is because 2+8 equals 10.

We have now determined that during this period of seven the east is an excellent location for your water feature. You can stop your analysis here and proceed to build your fishpond or waterfall in the east sector of your garden. It will be very auspicious.

However, to discover the exact magical spot in the house that benefits the most from a water feature – i.e. where water brings the greatest good luck – it is necessary to take the analysis further. For this you need to refer to the flying star natal chart of the house. And from the natal chart all you need to do is locate where the auspicious water star is. In the period of seven the auspicious water star is where the number 7 is located. But since the period of seven is now coming to a close the energy of the number 7 is weakening so it is the water star 8 that will bring the greatest benefit.

48. TIPS ON WATER PLACEMENT AND WATER FLOWS

- *It is important to note that when you place water features in your home or building for purposes of feng shui, the water should always be seen to be flowing in and never flowing out. Out-flowing water carries your wealth away while in-flowing water brings wealth into the home. This is a tip worth remembering when assessing the benefits of the natural water flow of rivers and canals.*

- When you build any water feature in your garden which taps the auspicious water stars in your natal chart, it is important to have a door or a window facing that water feature. This is what brings the all-important water chi into your home. A door is better than a window but only if it is kept open. If the door is kept closed all the time the beneficial chi will not be able to flow into the home.

- In feng shui one can differentiate between big water (natural water) and small water (man-made water). Generally the energy of big water is always stronger than small water but when there is no natural water around, man-made water is better than nothing.

- Water flow is different from a water feature. There are formulas on water flows that indicate the auspicious exit flow directions of water in the Yellow Emperor's Water Dragon Classic. Luck from water flows is different from luck that comes from water features.

- The basic rule about water flow is that when the house faces a cardinal direction (north, south, east, or west) water should flow past the front door from left to right. And when the house is facing a secondary direction (northeast, southeast, northwest, and southwest) the water should flow pass the front door from right to left.

- If you decide to install a waterfall in your garden (this is an especially excellent wealth energizer) ensure two things are observed: first that the water flows towards the house and there is a door to receive the water and second, let the water flow down six levels as this indicates that water is coming from heaven.

- When there is a river flowing past the front of the house it is said to be exceptionally auspicious if the river has the following three characteristics:

  1 When the river that flows past your house and the water comes into view from three different directions and then collects in front of the building. This happens usually when there are two other rivers pouring the water into the river that flows past your house. This creates the auspicious "three sources water." To maximize the benefit there should be a door to symbolically receive the water chi.

  2 When the river flows past the house as though the water is embracing the house – this signifies the "jade belt." Such water brings prosperity, power, and influence, especially when the surrounding hills also reflects the green dragon white tiger formation and there is a tortoise hill behind. The jade belt water brings great wealth.

  3 When the river flows towards the house and enters into view when very broad, then settles gently in front in full view of the house's main entrance. It then slowly gets narrower before tapering into a narrow stream flowing away. This arrangement of natural water suggests some wealth has been deposited by the river, making it a very auspicious feature.

風
水

Changing to Period Eight

**P
A
R
T

S
E
V
E
N**

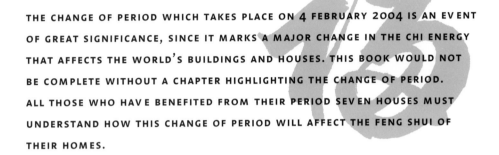

THE CHANGE OF PERIOD WHICH TAKES PLACE ON 4 FEBRUARY 2004 IS AN EVENT OF GREAT SIGNIFICANCE, SINCE IT MARKS A MAJOR CHANGE IN THE CHI ENERGY THAT AFFECTS THE WORLD'S BUILDINGS AND HOUSES. THIS BOOK WOULD NOT BE COMPLETE WITHOUT A CHAPTER HIGHLIGHTING THE CHANGE OF PERIOD. ALL THOSE WHO HAVE BENEFITED FROM THEIR PERIOD SEVEN HOUSES MUST UNDERSTAND HOW THIS CHANGE OF PERIOD WILL AFFECT THE FENG SHUI OF THEIR HOMES.

Remember, your house or building does not change period automatically. If you live in a period seven house it continues to be a period seven house until you take specific action to change it into a period eight house. How one should go about instigating this change is an issue that has generated some controversy. Most of the debate, however, centers around the extent of "renovation" needed to change the period of a building. Many agree that this renovation must include work on changing the roof of the house and that only by doing this will fresh new energy flow into the home. This opinion holds that this is the only way for new period chi of heaven and earth to connect. I am slightly less stringent on the roof requirements (see page 112). However, to change the period chi of your house from period seven to period eight, it is generally agreed that it is necessary to undertake fairly major renovations to your house as soon as we enter period eight.

Those living in apartment buildings might consider organizing a meeting of all residents to do something about changing the period of the building to a period eight building if they collectively agree that will benefit all residents.

Whether or not a building will have "better" luck if it were transformed into a period eight building depends on what the period eight natal chart looks like. So included in this chapter are the 16 flying star natal charts of period eight. Please note that the chart for houses and buildings facing the three sub-directions of southwest do not follow the original formula as given in the chapter on how flying charts are cast. This is because in the base period eight chart the 8 in the center means the number 5 has flown into the southwest palace. Note that the number 5 star does not have a fixed Yin or Yang pattern. Thus it assumes the Yin/Yang character of the palace that it occupies in any period. So it flies Yin (minus) or Yang (plus) according to the palace that it occupies.

In period seven the 5 star was in the east (which originally houses the 3 star) so it stays an odd number flying Yang, Yin, Yin (plus, minus, minus). In period eight, however, the number 5 has flown to the southwest which in the original Lo Shu grid houses the 2 star, which is an even number. So in period eight, the 5 star flies Yin, Yang, Yang or minus, plus, plus. This will therefore affect the natal chart numbers of houses that are built or renovated in the period of eight and are facing the southwest.

One of the most potent arguments for changing your home into a period eight house is that as soon as the period changes, all period seven houses immediately suffer from an instant weakening of chi. It is as if the chi that sustained them for the past 20 years has died. Also, the number 7 itself, which is generally regarded as a violent star number bringing violence and loss, reverts to its evil nature and turns malevolent. In the 20 years from 1984 to 2004 the 7 is the prominent star because these are the years of the seven period and this caused its usually malevolent energy to become auspicious during that time. As soon as period eight takes over, the 7 star becomes exceedingly unlucky and brings armed robbery and violence. It is therefore necessary to be very aware of this.

If you look at period seven charts you will find that many have the double 7 in their facing and back palaces. These houses must consider the option of changing their homes to period eight homes very seriously. They should plan for this change now since there are taboos regarding the renovations of houses. If you remember, there are annual afflictions in the form of the Five Yellow, the Grand Duke Jupiter, and the Three Killings that afflict different parts of the house from year to year. Thus if you want to make renovations it is vital to plan with these afflictions in mind since disturbing them will also bring misfortune. If you really have no choice, however, just make sure you never begin or end your renovations in sectors that are affected by any one of these three afflictions.

Here are the period eight charts which you can use to compare with your period seven charts
(see page 120). Work out how the chi of your house will change and how you can best redo
your house to tap into the luck of the period of eight.

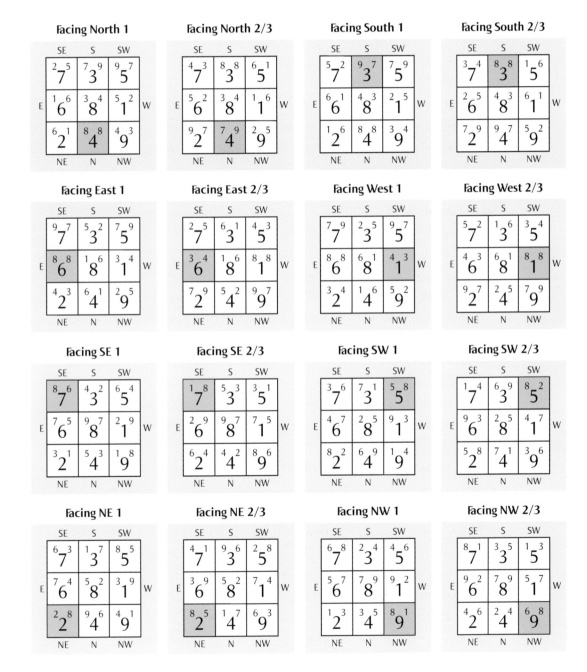

If you look at the period seven chart on the facing page for a house facing north 2/3, you will see that the occupants of this house must definitely consider changing its period to that of period eight because the main door is located in the palace with the double seven. This is extremely beneficial in the period of seven and residents have been benefiting from the double 7 since 1984. However, with the chi of 7 on the wane it is now vital for the feng shui of this house to be redone.

The residents need to plan how best they can take advantage of the star numbers indicated by the period eight chart. What is obvious is that if the change does take place, the facing palace of a north 2/3 house will have the mountain/water combination of 7/9 which does not indicate auspicious luck. Therefore it looks like the period eight chart for a north 2/3 house does not have an auspicious facing palace. But look at what happens when we use the north 1 chart below. In period eight if we use the renovation to tilt the door slightly and change its facing direction from north 2/3 to north 1, the facing palace will benefit from the mountain/water combination of double 8 which is enormously lucky.

The period eight chart of a north 1 house illustrated below shows the double 8 in the facing palace. This is one of the luckiest indications. However, also note that by changing the period of the house and then tilting the door, the master bedroom, which benefits from the 8/6 combination in period seven, now has to cope with very unlucky star numbers under the new period eight chart. If you look at the chart for a north 1 house you will find that the numbers of the palace where the master bedroom is located are 9, 5, and 7 – all very bad numbers and a combination that indicates loss, violence, and illness. So to benefit from the period and the wonderful double 8 in the facing palace it is necessary to install cures in the bedroom. To

House Facing N1

	SE	S	SW	
	2 5 **7**	7 9 **3**	9 7 **5**	
E	1 6 **6**	3 4 **8**	5 2 **1**	W
	6 1 **2**	8 8 **4**	4 3 **9**	
	NE	N	NW	

House facing North 2

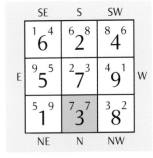

Period 7 chart

Period 8 chart

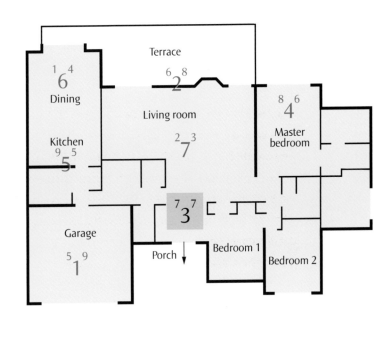

control the 9/7 combination the master bedroom will have to be decorated in shades of blue which indicate Yin water – do not use actual water! A blue bedroom will control the 9 mountain star and weaken the 7 water star. The rest of the house should also be carefully analyzed to compare the different chi distribution under period eight.

This then is Flying Star, or Shuan Kong, feng shui. For those of you interested in taking your knowledge of this wonderful system of feng shui further, it is a good idea to read other reference books on the subject. There is, however, no need to get too academic about this subject. What is more important than classical references are the practical aspects and applications of flying star. So interpretations of flying star methods must be undertaken in the context of today's modern environment. As with all sciences, metaphysical, esoteric, or otherwise, feng shui must keep up with a changing world.

風水

Lunar Calendars

APPENDIX

ANIMAL	WESTERN CALENDAR DATES
RAT (water)	Feb 18, 1912 – Feb 5, 1913
OX (earth)	Feb 6, 1913 – Jan 25, 1914
TIGER (wood)	Jan 26, 1914 – Feb 13 ,1915
RABBIT (wood)	Feb 14, 1915 – Feb 2, 1916
DRAGON (earth)	Feb 3, 1916 – Jan 22, 1917
SNAKE (fire)	Jan 23, 1917 – Feb 10, 1918
HORSE (fire)	Feb 11, 1918 – Jan 31, 1919
SHEEP (earth)	Feb 1, 1919 – Feb 19, 1920
MONKEY (metal)	Feb 20, 1920 – Feb 7, 1921
ROOSTER (metal)	Feb 8, 1921 – Jan 27, 1922
DOG (earth)	Feb 28, 1922 – Feb 15, 1923
BOAR (water)	Feb 16, 1923 – Feb 4, 1924

ANIMAL	WESTERN CALENDAR DATES

* start of 60 year Cycle

ANIMAL	WESTERN CALENDAR DATES
RAT (water)	Feb 5, 1924 – Jan 23, 1925
OX (earth)	Jan 24, 1925 – Feb 12, 1926
TIGER (wood)	Feb 13, 1926 – Feb 1, 1927
RABBIT (wood)	Feb 2, 1927 – Jan 22, 1928
DRAGON (earth)	Jan 23, 1928 – Feb 9, 1929
SNAKE (fire)	Feb 10, 1929 – Jan 29, 1930
HORSE (fire)	Jan 30, 1930 – Feb 16, 1931
SHEEP (earth)	Feb 17, 1931 – Feb 5, 1932
MONKEY (metal)	Feb 6, 1932 – Jan 25, 1933
ROOSTER (metal)	Jan 26, 1933 – Feb 13, 1934
DOG (earth)	Feb 14, 1934 – Feb 3, 1935
BOAR (water)	Feb 4, 1935 – Jan 23, 1936

ANIMAL	WESTERN CALENDAR DATES
RAT (water)	Jan 24, 1936 – Feb 10, 1937
OX (earth)	Feb 11, 1937 – Jan 30, 1938
TIGER (wood)	Jan 31, 1938 – Feb 18, 1939
RABBIT (wood)	Feb 19, 1939 – Feb 7, 1940
DRAGON (earth)	Feb 8, 1940 – Jan 26, 1941
SNAKE (fire)	Jan 27, 1941 – Feb 14, 1942
HORSE (fire)	Feb 15, 1942 – Feb 4, 1943
SHEEP (earth)	Feb 5, 1943 – Jan 24, 1944
MONKEY (metal)	Jan 25, 1944 – Feb 12, 1945
ROOSTER (metal)	Feb 13, 1945 – Feb 1, 1946
DOG (earth)	Feb 2, 1946 – Jan 21, 1947
BOAR (water)	Jan 22, 1947 – Feb 9, 1948

ANIMAL   WESTERN CALENDAR DATES

ANIMAL	WESTERN CALENDAR DATES
RAT (water)	Feb 10, 1948 – Jan 28, 1949
OX (earth)	Jan 29, 1949 – Feb 16, 1950
TIGER (wood)	Feb 17, 1950 – Feb 5, 1951
RABBIT (wood)	Feb 6, 1951 – Jan 26, 1952
DRAGON (earth)	Jan 27, 1952 – Feb 13, 1953
SNAKE (fire)	Feb 14, 1953 – Feb 2, 1954
HORSE (fire)	Feb 3, 1954 – Jan 23, 1955
SHEEP (earth)	Jan 24, 1955 – Feb 11, 1956
MONKEY (metal)	Feb 12 ,1956 – Jan 30, 1957
ROOSTER (metal)	Jan 31, 1957 – Feb 17, 1958
DOG (earth)	Feb 18, 1958 – Feb 7, 1959
BOAR (water)	Feb 8, 1959 – Jan 27, 1960

ANIMAL	WESTERN CALENDAR DATES
RAT (water)	Jan 28, 1960 – Feb 14, 1961
OX (earth)	Feb 15, 1961 – Feb 4, 1962
TIGER (wood)	Feb 5, 1962 – Jan 24, 1963
RABBIT (wood)	Jan 25, 1963 – Feb 12, 1964
DRAGON (earth)	Feb 13, 1964 – Feb 1, 1965
SNAKE (fire)	Feb 2, 1965 – Jan 20, 1966
HORSE (fire)	Jan 21, 1966 – Feb 8, 1967
SHEEP (earth)	Feb 9, 1967 – Jan 29, 1968
MONKEY (metal)	Jan 30, 1968 – Feb 16, 1969
ROOSTER (metal)	Feb 17, 1969 – Feb 5, 1970
DOG (earth)	Feb 6, 1970 – Jan 26, 1971
BOAR (water)	Jan 27, 1971 – Feb 14, 1972

ANIMAL	WESTERN CALENDAR DATES
RAT (water)	Feb 15, 1972 – Feb 2, 1973
OX (earth)	Feb 3, 1973 – Jan 22, 1974
TIGER (wood)	Jan 23, 1974 – Feb 10, 1975
RABBIT (wood)	Feb 11, 1975 – Jan 30, 1976
DRAGON (earth)	Jan 31, 1976 – Feb 17, 1977
SNAKE (fire)	Feb 18, 1977 – Feb 6, 1978
HORSE (fire)	Feb 7, 1978 – Jan 27, 1979
SHEEP (earth)	Jan 28, 1979 – Feb 15, 1980
MONKEY (metal)	Feb 16, 1980 – Feb 4, 1981
ROOSTER (metal)	Feb 5, 1981 – Jan 24, 1982
DOG (earth)	Jan 25, 1982 – Feb 12, 1983
BOAR (water)	Feb 13, 1983 – Feb 1, 1984

* Start of 60 year cycle

RAT (water)	Feb 2, 1984 – Feb 19, 1985
OX (earth)	Feb 20, 1985 – Feb 8, 1986
TIGER (wood)	Feb 9, 1986 – Jan 28, 1987
RABBIT (wood)	Jan 29, 1987 – Feb 16, 1988
DRAGON (earth)	Feb 17, 1988 – Feb 5, 1989
SNAKE (fire)	Feb 6, 1989 – Jan 26, 1990
HORSE (fire)	Jan 27, 1990 – Feb 14, 1991
SHEEP (earth)	Feb 15, 1991 – Feb 3, 1992
MONKEY (metal)	Feb 4, 1992 – Jan 22, 1993
ROOSTER (metal)	Jan 23, 1993 – Feb 9, 1994
DOG (earth)	Feb 10, 1994 – Jan 30, 1995
BOAR (water)	Jan 31, 1995 – Feb 18, 1996

ANIMAL

WESTERN CALENDAR DATES

RAT (water)	Feb 19, 1996 – Feb 6, 1997
OX (earth)	Feb 7, 1997 – Jan 27, 1998
TIGER (wood)	Jan 28, 1998 – Feb 15, 1999
RABBIT (wood)	Feb 16, 1999 – Feb 4, 2000
DRAGON (earth)	Feb 5, 2000 – Jan 23, 2001
SNAKE (fire)	Jan 24, 2001 – Feb 11, 2002
HORSE (fire)	Feb 12, 2002 – Jan 31, 2003
SHEEP (earth)	Feb 1, 2003 – Jan 21, 2004
MONKEY (metal)	Jan 22, 2004 – Feb 8, 2005
ROOSTER (metal)	Feb 9, 2005 – Jan 28, 2006
DOG (earth)	Jan 29, 2006 – Feb 17, 2007
BOAR (water)	Feb 18, 2007 – Feb 6, 2008

風
水

Index

IN THIS INDEX ONLY PERIOD EIGHT HOUSES ARE SPECIFIED AS SUCH. ALL OTHER HOUSES REFER TO PERIOD SEVEN.